UNLEASH INTENTIONAL SUCCESS

UNLEASH INTENTIONAL SUCCESS

CHANGE YOUR MINDSET.
CHANGE YOUR ACTIONS.
CHANGE YOUR LIFE.

Namaine Coombs

Magnificent Life Publishing,
An imprint of Unleashed Success, LLC

Unleash Intentional Success: Change Your Mindset. Change Your Actions. Change Your Life.

First edition, March 2021

ISBN: 978-1-7346889-0-0 (hardback)
ISBN: 978-1-7346889-1-7 (paperback)
ISBN: 978-1-7346889-2-4 (e-book)
Library of Congress Control Number: 2021906812

Editing: Shayla Raquel, shaylaraquel.com
Cover Design: Rina Pal, rinapal50@gmail.com
Interior Formatting: Sarah Lange Davis & Team, eliteauthors.com

Unleashed Success, LLC
9716 Rea Rd
Ste B PMB 1011
Charlotte, NC 28277

namainecoombs.com

For Mom and Dad, who gave me their best.

Table of Contents

Foreword

FOR NEARLY FIFTEEN years, I spent my career in marketing and communications. In the fall of 2019, as Namaine and I sat at the bar of a darkly lit restaurant in uptown Charlotte, I was sharing with him my aspirations of completely scrapping the career I had built my name, life, and goals on. I sought to become a domestic violence and motherhood life coach, speaker, and corporate consultant. And I wanted to take him up on being my accountability partner.

I met Namaine just a couple of years ago through a—*gasp!*—ex-boyfriend. The ex-boyfriend shared with me that Namaine was this well-respected VP at a large bank in the city. Later, I learned that Namaine ran marathons, played golf, was an avid traveler, and sat on the board of directors for a local Charlotte school. I was impressed! Although my relationship with my boyfriend ended, Namaine and I still kept in touch.

Prior to that evening at the restaurant, I knew in order to accomplish this new life, I would need to do some serious mindset work, let go of procrastination, set my intentions, and get uncomfortable. I desired to make an amount of money that I had always dreamed of but thought was out of reach. I had to release old habits, thoughts, and patterns. I needed the blueprint. I knew I couldn't do it alone.

In my more than twenty-year work history, I've never had an accountability partner. Sure, I've had one for working out, but even that didn't last longer than two months. One of the suggestions for seeking an accountability partner is for this person to have similar values as you. What I wanted in an accountability partner was someone who was already successful, made more money than me, would be brutally honest at times, and was willing to take time out of their busy schedule to get my behind in gear. Most important to this dynamic was my need not to feel judged by where I was then in my life.

One day after meditation, I took stock of who I knew that fit that criteria. Immediately, Namaine came to mind. I told myself, "Why would he want to be an accountability partner to the ex-girlfriend of his friend? He's too busy, and I'm not on his level." Although he offered, I still had my hesitation. I almost let fear take over. As we dined on that delicious food, I asked, with bated breath, "I was wondering if you have any interest in being my accountability partner? I read this is great to have, especially when you're starting a new journey. You're one of the most successful people I know and well, I understand if you're too busy . . ." I tend to ramble when I'm nervous.

And yet in his cool, relaxed, always-at-ease personality and tone, he said, "I offered, so let's do it."

Jackpot!

Every other week, Namaine and I met and set our intentions. We had weekly check-ins and shared resources. When I shared that I had found a coaching certification program, Namaine shared he was looking for one. The next week, we were in class together. To this day, when I'm having moments of self-doubt, Namaine reminds me why I'm on this journey and not to let fear take over. His presence is the reminder that "repetition, consistency, and support are the keys to lasting healing, change, and growth."

In *Unleash Intentional Success,* Namaine takes you on a journey of self-discovery. While reading his book, you'll have many aha moments. You'll think, "Ugh, that's totally me" or "Do I really need to address that feeling?" or "I needed to hear that!" This book is *not* for you if you're not ready to get uncomfortable, address the ugly, and try something new.

It's *not* for you if you aren't ready to talk about how you self-sabotage your success. If you're settled with playing the victim, this book is not for you. If you want to continue to play small and not go after your true desires, just gift this book to someone who *is* ready.

Unleash Intentional Success is for you if you want to get rid of your limiting beliefs, practice self-love and self-care, take action, be present, make money, manifest your life, and live your purpose. While reading, take notes, use a highlighter, circle paragraphs, journal, or write Post-it notes. Get out of it all you can use in your daily life.

I am honored to have Namaine as not just my accountability partner but also as my friend. Seeing his journey to writing *Unleash Intentional Success* is inspiring. My wish is for you to be inspired, motivated, and moved to action. My desire is for you to experience success unlike anything you've ever experienced.

—Melody Gross,
Advocate, Speaker, Writer, Life Coach, and Founder of Courageous Shift

Introduction

"An unintentional life accepts everything and does nothing. An intentional life embraces only the things that will add to the mission of significance."
—John C. Maxwell

THERE ARE MOMENTS when we perceive obstacles that block us from happiness and success in life. Perhaps it's your job, age, intelligence, money, health, marriage, faith, or even childhood. We find comfort within ourselves by placing blame, projecting resentment, and misplacing judgment on others. These perceptions become our realities as we become resistant to change through procrastination, perfectionism, and self-sabotaging behavior.

People apply Band-Aids instead of healing and commit to fixes instead of solutions. I perceive this as truth and accept that we modify our actions to change our circumstances but not our beliefs to improve decisions, thoughts, actions, or outcomes.

God, the universe, cocreator, spiritual connection, or whatever you believe in has a way of getting our attention through restlessness, distractions, disappointments, and disruptions when a life change needs to occur. It's up to us to be aware of the messages and follow the path of least resistance to intentional or purposeful change. The 11,536th message (give or take) provided to me was an internal struggle with depression and anxiety followed by an official diagnosis.

Often, it's not until we reach the brink of despair that we become inspired to achieve ultimate contentment. As a person who wanted to be joyful and thriving more than anything, I refused to be defined by mental health conditions. A problem that I perceived needed to be fixed.

My quest to prove that people, including me, can eternally change morphed into a remarkable transformation. It blossomed into an awakened growth journey that began with mastering the inner workings of my conscious and subconscious minds. I scrutinized and investigated why permanent change or living in the present is cumbersome for many of us. I connected with subject matter experts on the brain's limbic system, the part of the brain responsible for regulating our emotions and motivations. More importantly, I identified and practiced methods to intentionally evolve my emotions, beliefs, and behaviors to achieve greater happiness and success. Living in alignment with my values, beliefs, and goals and rejecting everything that conflicts with a success mindset positioned me to positively contribute to myself and others. A victorious intentional subconscious evolution unleashed higher levels of self-love, mindfulness, self-healing, a progressive mindset, and intentional actions that changed my life!

And I want that for you too.

Thanks to my growth journey, my happiness and success come from within and are continually reaching levels far beyond my imagination every day. I reclaimed my mental and physical health, strengthened flourishing relationships, nurtured my spirituality, earned a promotion at work, wrote a book, became a certified professional coach, and advocate for mental health. Consider the boundless possibilities *you* can invite into your life by intentionally evolving your emotions, beliefs, and behaviors. You have the power to unleash more than you can mentally conceive! I humbly come before you to inspire and guide you through intentional change as you embark on your growth journey to unleash intentional success and happiness. I want you to be joyful and triumphant in your life!

Before we begin to discuss where we're going, we have to understand how we got here. From the womb to several years after birth, the information we receive, purposefully and haphazardly, defines our fundamental beliefs. My parents, grandparents, siblings, playmates, teachers, babysitters, and more influenced who I became. Observations, opinions, biases, and experiences subconsciously swayed how I see the world. The teachings, expectations, and approvals of others navigated my thoughts and actions as I developed my views. Mom told me to trust my gut, so I trusted my gut. Dad told me that I'm not to eat pork, so I didn't eat pork.

As we became young adults, we critique, confirm, and reject information to refine our underlying beliefs and perceptions of reality. We begin to untie from our beginnings and assess the world for ourselves! Some of us develop a life of happiness and success while others remain on a continual search. Either way, how do we know what happiness and success look like? Is our measure of happiness and success based on an expectation or approval? Were happiness and success defined for us? Maybe happiness and success are what we see on television or social media. (Just kidding.) How do we find happiness and success for ourselves?

Information sent our way can subconsciously limit our thoughts and actions and create hurdles for our happiness and success. You've probably heard as a youngster, "Pursue a craft or profession that makes money, such as a doctor, engineer, or lawyer." Does that mean no other career makes money? "Drop the football. The chances of making it to the National Football League are slim." Could you have made it to the NFL without this limiting belief embedded in your subconscious mind? Or how about this: "Focus on a better career path since you don't have what it takes to be a fashion model." Just because it didn't work for the person who said that does not mean it won't work for you. Oh, and my favorite: "You need to have a college education to be successful." What if Steve Jobs or Bill Gates continued with the belief that college was necessary to be successful? Would they have been the society-changing pioneers of the tech giant companies we are familiar with today?

Limitations justified by limiting beliefs are prevalent and constrain our ability to see the whole enchilada of possibilities! How many more free-thinkers, leaders, influencers, entrepreneurs, inventors, musicians, artists, visionaries, athletes, and more would there be without limiting beliefs? For crying out loud, the basic concept of the internal combustion engine used in vehicles today is similar to the design of the 1800s. Is Elon Musk the only person with limitless beliefs to have made notable advancements in alternatively powering personal cars since the 1800s?

How have subconsciously biased or inherited beliefs limited you? Fortunately for you, we can work together to replace limiting beliefs and inspire intentional actions that can invite unprecedented levels of happiness and success into your life. When we intentionally unleash our full potential, anything is possible! In *Unleash Intentional Success*, I share personal stories, teach concepts, provide guidance, and recommend practices to expand happiness and success. The information provided on each page is just information. It's up to you to be emotionally open and mentally aware and become empowered by the stories and concepts. This book invites you to consider life-changing practices to upgrade your life as you self-reflect. You define your happiness and success.

This book is here to help you unleash limitless beliefs and provide guidance based on one man's journey of growth. Our struggles may vary, but we all can make deliberate decisions to be intentionally happy and successful for ourselves. If you want greater happiness and success in your life, you must do more than read the words on the pages. Feel the thoughts and concepts as they emerge from each page and intentionally direct your attention to applying the learnings to your life. Reread sentences, paragraphs, pages, chapters, and sections to get the most out of this book. Take notes! Repetition, consistency, and support are the keys to lasting healing, change, and growth. Let's do the work together to unleash intentional success by changing your mindset, actions, and life!

PART I
Change Your Mindset

CHAPTER ONE

Living in the Absence of Light

"Reality is a projection of your thoughts of the things you habitually think about."
—Stephen Richards

DAD WAS MY life teacher, an everyman hero, and a role model of what I aspired to be as I matriculated through life.

As a youngster, I eagerly awaited Dad's arrival from work, cried when he was not around, and constantly tried to escape behind him as he exited our home to do whatever it was that adults did. I revered him, and he pushed me to see beyond what was in front of me, to be the best person I could be at all times, and to live passionately. Without understanding the depth of Dad's influence on my beliefs and thoughts, I became attached to his expectations and approval.

I moved like him, thought like him, and yearned for his attention. He picked up running as his choice of exercise, so I picked up running. He liked German cars, so I liked German cars. We were two peas in a pod, and many people would even say we look just alike.

Dad was a commissioned officer in the U.S. Army and often shared stories of how the military helped him create a successful life and provided for his family in ways that he had never imagined. For this reason and many others, I developed a fondness for the opportunities for success that joining the military could provide. I was unsure if I would join the military before or after college, but I was reasonably sure the military was for me.

As I approached the latter years of high school, Dad encouraged me to focus on my grades and get accepted into the West Point Military Academy or enter the military after high school. Since he knew military movies, fighter planes, and famous battleships intrigued me, Dad felt the military would provide a bright and promising future for me as the army had provided for him. I applied to my top three college choices and attended the University of South Carolina, delaying my military entry.

During college, I attended career-readiness programs in the business school and applied to the U.S. Marine Officer Candidate School in Quantico, VA. Through two tough six-week summer sessions, Sargent Instructors are tasked with evaluating officer candidates based on their character and ability to lead peers under uncertain and chaotic conditions.

I attended the first session of OCS and was one of a few remaining officer candidates who graduated. My family attended the graduation ceremony. Dad, dressed in uniform, approached me as I relinquished my military-issued M-16 rifle to the armory. I adhered to traditional military custom and saluted Dad as I would any other commissioned officer. While I stood there firmly at attention, eyes locked forward with a firm hand placed centimeters from my brow, you might expect my proud and devoted father with over two decades of military service to return a warm customary salute. Well, you'd be wrong.

Instead, Dad broke his typical stoic facial expression with the brightest smile and securely hugged me like no other time before. The twelve-second embrace between father and son, both dressed in uniform, seemed like an eternity and became a defining moment that would forever change us both.

After such an enlightening and emotional military experience, my beliefs and thoughts about the meaning of success shifted. I felt compelled to reassess my passions and purpose. I gained strength in understanding my potential for greatness. As I reflected on OCS and the graduation ceremony, I realized the military had inherently become my measure for success through Dad's experiences. The OCS journey removed limiting subconscious beliefs and placed me on a mission to define success for myself.

Dad's beliefs became my beliefs, but that was far from his intentions. The military was Dad's secret sauce for success, and he offered the best of his wisdom and experiences to help position me to succeed in life as any caring parent would. As reenforced by his disinterest in my salute, Dad was less concerned about whether I entered the military and more concerned with whether I was happy and prosperous doing whatever I wanted to do.

The twelve-second hug back in Quantico was not a military father and son embracing and basking in their common interest. The embrace symbolized a proud dad seeing his son happy and motivated. Dad understood the program's difficulty, challenges and was as much a part of the victory as his son.

The following college semester became a stage for focus and growth. I stepped out from Dad's shadow and began discovering my light. I viewed the world through my eyes and unveiled a passion for finance. The more aware I became of my values and passions, the more my career outlook evolved. I could succeed at anything, and my parents would be proud no matter what I chose to do to be successful. I set intentions and goals and executed action plans to prepare myself to be recruited and work in the finance industry after college graduation. To start, I garnered a part-time job in banking.

Without knowing our values, passions, and purpose, we decide our actions based on expectations, experiences, and observations that live within our subconscious mind. Values are core principles such as kindness, self-respect, or service that are important to us and determine our character, mindset, and behavior. If we don't commit to our values, we become chameleons, blending in with society with little sense of direction. We become influenced simply by others and our environments. Peter Marshall, Scottish Clergyman, notes, "If you don't stand for something you will fall for anything."

Many of us struggle as we venture through life to understand who we are, our values, and what we want. Flawed beliefs or ideas limit us. Do you know where your thoughts come from? Are your opinions based on your views or reasoning from your influences? Let's take a moment to discuss the conscious and subconscious minds to illustrate how we limit our maximum potential for success through our beliefs, thoughts, and actions.

Our conscious mind is our current awareness and delivers creativity, dwells on the past, and carries out actions. The conscious mind thinks about your next meal as you are driving down the highway. Our subconscious mind evokes instinctive and developed behaviors, emotions, imagination, gut intuition, and essential involuntary functions of the body such as breathing. The subconscious mind says steer left or right and locates the gas and brake pedals without focused thought. Many of us would assume the conscious mind influences our daily behavior. This assumption is a common misconception. The conscious mind processes a single thought at a time and has minimal memory. The subconscious mind feeds information to the conscious mind and determines almost all of our behavior.

The subconscious mind begins its development by gathering information from the latter stages of womb life and continues through childhood before we analyze, consider, and critique information. Our brain, where the conscious and subconscious minds reside, has not fully developed at this point in life. We are like sponges subconsciously absorbing all information without validation. The guidance of our communities contribute to our belief system and provide the foundation of who we become. As we age, we reject information that does not align with our beliefs and confirm information that supports what we have learned, experienced, and observed.

Not all information presented, passed along, or observed creates quality beliefs or thoughts that align with our values. The subconscious mind knows no difference between the quality and validity of the information. Information is just information. Throughout our lifetimes, we come into our own by refining our belief system, creating what we may believe to be our own lives, and seeking experiences and guidance beyond our early influences. If we're not aware of how our belief system came to be or that our beliefs may be flawed, we may self-sabotage or obstruct ourselves from building meaningful relationships and thriving with fulfillment—the ability to be happy and satisfied through the process or journey.

Self-sabotaging behaviors interrupt, delay, and prevent progress toward what we want. We may say we want a promotion at work but exhibit self-sabotaging behaviors with tardiness or doing the minimum to get by. We may have a great business idea but sabotage turning the concept into reality with procrastination or lack of focus. We may want to be millionaires but sabotage by overspending or making poor investment decisions. Many of us are aware of our thoughts but are not observant of the beliefs that influence them. If we do not evaluate the sources and validity of our thoughts and actions, we wander through life feeling unaware of who we are and unknowingly sabotage our lives. We may find ourselves on a tireless external search for happiness, attaching to people, places, or things instead of refining our mindset and behavior for better outcomes.

Are you searching for happiness?

What if I told you that happiness is within you? Would you believe me? If we don't know who we are, how can we know what makes us happy? Our childhood learnings and observations define success, love, happiness, and a good life and career for us, which become the foundation for our views and experiences as we grow into adults. Your child-rearing influences have raised you with their beliefs, enabling and limiting, and it is up to you to redefine those beliefs for yourself to achieve the level of happiness and success that is for you. Everything that is for them is for them, and everything that is for you is for you.

Have you clarified to yourself what happiness and success looks like for you—not what it looks like to your family or friends?

We subconsciously lean on our limiting beliefs to justify limited happiness or success, such as the common thought, "I'm too old to change." Maybe someone told you once that artists never make money, so you pushed aside the idea of becoming an artist. What if you could have been an artist contracted by large corporations or opened a profitable art gallery and made top dollar for the value you deliver on canvas? Nothing stops you from being the great artist you are except a subconscious limiting belief. You will never know how far you can go until you replace limiting beliefs with limit*less* beliefs. Understanding the underlying beliefs of the subconscious mind that limit our happiness is critical to maximizing our full potential as human beings.

Ingrained belief limitations lead us to live our lives as victims or feel entitled based on what we have been provided, shown, taught, and encountered. Perhaps you were raised homeless, lived among violence, or had daddy issues. Does a colorful childhood mean your full potential to be successful or serve others is any less? Only if you believe so. Nobody had the perfect childhood, Buttercup. There is no correlation between our childhoods and level of success when we dispose of the subconscious beliefs that limit our perceived realities. Jay-Z, Oprah Winfrey, Robert Downey Jr., Tony Robbins, and Tyler Perry all had less-than-perfect childhoods. They had their respective struggles but did not allow early circumstances to weigh on their happiness, aspirations for success, or limit who they could become.

Our mindset and thoughts cannot provide avenues for successful action if negative or tainted information drives our decision-making. Garbage in leads to garbage out. We can take out the trash and live our best lives by the intentions we set and actions we take. Set intentions by making a purposeful decision to direct emotions, focus, and actions to complete a task or executing a plan or goal. Intention setting is a potent way to support positive thought and action in achieving the success you desire. Everything that is remarkable or accomplished began with intention. A seed has the intention to bear fruit. An embryo has the intention to be a human. Is your idea of success based on your passions and values?

What will it take for you to unleash your best self? Do you want more? Do you feel that the life you're living differs from the life you envisioned? Do you have the will to commit to put in the work and achieve growth?

Many of us experience life-changing awakenings or a sudden heightened level of self-awareness, leading to an internal disruption where we are no longer comfortable with the status quo. At different points in our lives, something or someone inspires us to launch or relaunch a journey of self-discovery, healing, and growth. We may aim to accomplish a goal perceived as complex, challenging, or perhaps different from anything we have ever attempted. Consider the forty-seven-year-old librarian who suddenly goes skydiving when the most daring thing he has ever done as an adult was to drink three glasses of wine on a work night.

A growth journey is an evolution of ourselves which can be scary since we are, knowingly or unknowingly, committing to pursue an unknown course of action to create better realities for ourselves. For Neo, in *The Matrix*, his growth journey began with the words, "Follow the white rabbit." Some of us do nothing when the start of a growth journey is right in front of us. We may view the path too complex, or not recognize that our awakened moment is here. Others feel the urge to answer the call but fear life disruptions and are comfortable with the familiar versus unknown.

A nagging internal discomfort can be continuously present when we are living out of alignment with our values and goals. We may reach for perceived life-changing experiences. Depending on when in our lives the awakened moment occurs, the restlessness or dissatisfaction could lead to the quintessential quarter (ages between early twenties and mid-thirties) or midlife (ages between late thirties and sixty-five crisis).

A quarter or midlife crisis is an emotional reach to discover who we are or why we are here, and what we are doing with our lives. The sheer uncertainty or loss of direction as we review our existence leads to faltering self-confidence and a revaluation of self-worth. I know what you're thinking; midlife is late to be reevaluating self-worth. It's never too late! Vera Wang, an American iconic fashion designer, began her career at age forty. Samuel L. Jackson did not receive his first significant movie role until he was forty. Colonel Sanders turned Kentucky Fried Chicken (KFC) into a franchise at the bright age of sixty-two.

Others of us that are going through a crisis may choose to get a sports car, hair plugs, plastic surgery, a hot new mate, or initiate a new workout routine to redefine ourselves. Does it work? Possibly, but external gratification leaves unaddressed ugly voids and limits our happiness, peace, and joy. An empty container is still an empty container no matter how much we dress up the outside of the container.

The catalyst for the change begins with an aha moment or lingering dissatisfaction spurred by a spiritual conversation, self-help book, life-changing event, breakup, someone you admire, a close death, or just about anything. Other times we find ourselves on paths to change through a chain of reactions or events without being consciously aware that a journey of change has begun. What was your aha moment?

Our perceived realities are reflections of our beliefs, thoughts, and actions. What we think about is what we invite into our lives. If we focus on emptiness or internalize feelings of lack, we are welcoming more emptiness and lack into our lives. When we focus on negativity, we invite more negativity. The judgment of others or ourselves is negative self-talk. Negative self-talk is the self-defeating dialogue we have with ourselves, such as "How can I be so stupid?" or "I should have never trusted her." Unless we are stupid, we are reinforcing the subconscious belief that we are stupid. If we tell ourselves that we should not have trusted someone, we are creating beliefs that limit relationships since trust in relationships would not be mutual. Negative thoughts or stories that plague our conscious minds constrain intentional success and positive outcomes. If we are spending time and energy judging others or ourselves, there is no space for positive emotions and thoughts to invite what we want into our lives.

Every minute we exert energy on negativity, we lose a minute of positive emotion and thought toward happiness, desires, and goals.

Would you be happier or further than you are today by being less negative? Negativity is a disguise for fear and insecurities. If you could influence the amount of happiness or success in your life, would you change how you feel, think, and act?

Influencing happiness and success comes down to three critical things:

1. Replacing limiting beliefs in the subconscious mind.
2. Setting the intention for success as you define success.
3. Having unconditional trust in the process.

What stories have you told yourself that have defined your life? What is your truth? Think about your mindset, actions, judgments, successes, and limitations. Are you proud of where and who you are, or is there more for you? The concept of unleashing intentional success centers on using the power of intention to evolve our mindset and actions to minimize self-sabotaging behavior to increase opportunities for greater happiness and success.

Growth begins when you let go of limiting beliefs and open your mind to new opportunities and limitless possibilities. Is today the day you start your growth journey? Growth and opportunity occur when we are no longer in our comfort zone. Let's get uncomfortable together and be a witness to your extraordinary transformation.

TIME FOR REFLECTION

My beliefs come from:

As a child, I learned about success and what it means from:

My definition of success is:

My self-sabotaging behaviors are:

My passions and purpose are:

CHAPTER TWO

There's a Program for That

"The way to get rid of darkness is with light; the way to overcome cold is with heat; the way to overcome the negative thought is to substitute the good thought. Affirm the good, and the bad will vanish."
—Joseph Murphy

THROUGHOUT LIFE, I have been fascinated with the Viking era and perceive Vikings to be the classic alpha male. Vikings had the mental toughness of a steel beam, Hercules' physical prowess, and the presence of a lion among gazelles in the Serengeti. Vikings feared nothing, not even death, and flourished in the harshest of conditions without a whimper.

I read many Viking stories and concluded that their primitive thinking ways would serve many of us value even today. Would a Viking multitask or focus on the task at hand? Would a Viking fear the future or dwell on the past? Would a Viking let neediness or lack consume his mental space? These thought-provoking questions can marinate with you for now.

Beyond big and burly men, the Viking Age introduced several magnificent and divine ships. Whether the vessels were for war or trade, they were remarkable and structured to carry troves of warriors into battle or plenty of goods for exchange. We can only wonder how the floating Viking fortresses stayed afloat. I shiver thinking about the long and brutal voyages across the Mediterranean Sea: choppy waters, treacherous weather conditions, scarcity of rations, no technology other than maybe a sundial, and rampant sea sicknesses and festering diseases.

The Viking vessel that interests me the most is the longship. The longship was long, slender, and probably the Viking Age's most recognizable ship, with over one hundred rowing positions and a notorious dragonhead on the vessel's front or bow. Hold a picture of the longship in mind as we use this vessel to help us understand how the subconscious mind can hamper success with limiting beliefs.

Vikings needed a vessel, skipper, rowing crew and row master, cooks, and seamen to set out to sail. Imagine the Viking vessel as your physical body, the rowing crew as your subconscious mind, and the row master as your conscious mind. To get the ship moving, the row master (conscious mind) calls out commands, probably in a degrading manner, to the rowing crew (subconscious mind) to commence rowing, sway steering and influence speed. No matter how fast the row master wanted the rowing crew to row, the rowing crew could only go as quickly as mentally prepared to execute on command. Since most, if not all, of the rowers were slaves or servants, the rowing crew was not the most enthusiastic bunch of comrades or motivated about the journey. Their focus was on survival and freedom and not in alignment with the row master's commands.

The row master has an objective as he sends commands. The rowing crew responds to the commands based on their limiting beliefs and thoughts, which leads to progress but limited progress. Let's suppose the rowing crew was just as determined about the voyage as the row master: Would the vessels arrive at destinations faster and maneuver more nimbly? I believe so. Have you pursued a goal with limited success? Perhaps the goal didn't align with your values, or there was subconscious fear or doubt.

The simplistic row master/rowing crew example helps us understand how vital our subconscious beliefs and thoughts determine the quality of our daily actions. We can significantly improve outcomes by reprogramming our subconscious minds to replace limiting beliefs and influence value-adding actions that lead to better results. If the rowing crew's views aligned with the commands of the row master, the rowing crew would exhibit higher levels of energy and consciousness leading to faster and more powerful rowing. The vessel would reach its destination with tremendous success.

Tuning into our conscious thoughts can enable us to observe our awareness in the present moment. The subconscious mind contains embedded attitudes, habits, and beliefs. We have the tools within us to change how we feel, believe, think, and act. Replacing limiting beliefs increases the probability of success by minimizing the misaligned thoughts and self-sabotaging behavior. We are capable of being who we want to be and having whatever we want.

Some examples of limiting beliefs are:

- "I do not deserve a promotion."
- "I'll never afford a house big enough for my family."
- "My family does not support my dreams."

Reprogramming the subconscious mind requires self-awareness. Self-awareness is being mindful of how our beliefs, emotions, and thoughts affect our actions. If we are not aware of feelings, beliefs, and thoughts, reprogramming the subconscious mind is impossible. Do you know the limiting messages that are in your subconscious mind? Very few of us are aware of our perceived limitations unless limiting thoughts and behaviors have been pointed out to us.

Some of us defend our thoughts and behavior rather than reevaluate our beliefs and actions. The subconscious messages become who we are, but they do not have to be. At times we attach ourselves to our beliefs and do not understand how our thoughts and behaviors are being affected. Without thoughts of fear or doubt, we can expand the subconscious mind to influence actions that deliver successful outcomes. We must reprogram the subconscious to buy into positivity and abundant beliefs and reject negativity and lack. Abundant or limitless beliefs enable us to reframe our thoughts to invite possibilities and support productive actions.

Some examples of limitless beliefs are:

- "I can earn a promotion."
- "I can create a plan to afford a big house for my family."
- "I support my dreams."

In the Viking vessel example, if the row master was aware of how the rowing crew's limiting beliefs negatively affected the journey, perhaps the row master could have inspired hope by using motivating commands or something to elevate their mindset. There are multiple ways to gain and raise self-awareness to reprogram the subconscious mind. Each method has its benefits. Achieving self-awareness is just the beginning of becoming a better version of yourself. Practicing self-awareness combined with positive daily habits, can establish productive thought and value-adding behaviors. Repetition and consistency are crucial to achieving favorable outcomes with any attempt at long-term change. As Jen Sincero says in her book, *You Are a Badass*, "You need to go from wanting to change your life to deciding to change your life."

REPROGRAMMING THE SUBCONSCIOUS MIND

In each chapter, I provide specific steps you can take to unleash intentional success. To start, I want you to work on reprogramming your subconscious mind. Remember that this cannot happen overnight. You must be patient and give yourself grace as you reconstruct your life's belief system.

1. Formulate intentions that align with your goals.
Setting an intention concentrates mental focus and emotional energy on the present and becomes the spark that propels us toward a goal. Being intentional is thinking and behaving with purposeful awareness. Intentions guide our thoughts and actions in alignment with our plans. Goals target a desired outcome or achievement.

Goal: I want to be a millionaire by age forty.
Intention: I intend to be wealthy.

The goal is the outcome, and the intention is your mental guide to align your thoughts and actions with your goal. See the difference?

Your thoughts and actions today must be in alignment to become wealthy and a millionaire. Start by believing that you have everything you need and spending in a manner that allows you to save money, build assets or generate income progressively.

An intention encourages feelings and emotions that influence your daily thoughts and behaviors. Our intentions or lack of intentions explain our realities. Intentions lay the mental bedrock that promotes a progressive mindset and deliberate actions toward our goals. If you could push the reset button and design a 2.0 version of your life, what would be different? What would you be willing to change about your thoughts and actions to materialize your new life? What we think about is what we become. Define intentions that resonate with your values and align with your goals. You are worthy, deserving, and capable of setting intentions and achieving anything you desire.

Beginning with a single intention simplifies the daunting long-term goal of reprogramming your subconscious mind. Develop an intention that you can easily recite and remember daily. Suppose your intention is "I intend to feel good about my body." Daily thoughts and habits upheld by the intention may include eating healthier and consistent exercise. Once you set an intention, increase your awareness of the quality of your thoughts and actions to confirm they are in agreement with your intention. Write down your intentions to make them real and easy to reference. Set a new intention when aligned thoughts and behaviors become instinctive, and you see the results.

2. Perceive to be real.

The subconscious mind is unaware of the difference between perception and reality, what we are seeing versus what is happening. Perception is the lens we look through to understand the world based on our beliefs, interpretation, and understanding. From an early presented through science books and the media have confirmed that the Earth is round. Suppose we had learned the Earth is flat, and our influences, observations, and experiences confirmed that the Earth is flat. Is the Earth round or flat? Whether the Earth is round or flat is irrelevant to the subconscious mind. If the subconscious mind is programmed to believe the Earth is flat, then our perceived reality suggests the Earth is flat.

Your perception is your reality. We can use this mental concept to our advantage by subconsciously picturing desired outcomes as if they have already occurred. If you see yourself as a CEO, then walk, talk, and make decisions like a CEO. Be the person you intend to be. Be the CEO of your life and align your actions with your values and objectives. Nobody can take a CEO mindset from you except you.

A success mindset—having the resilience to envision unlimited possibilities and action steps-aligned with intentional actions improves expected outcomes no matter how big or small. Does having a success mindset imply we should ignore or minimize disputes, setbacks, or obstacles? No! Success does not come without challenges. We must acknowledge problems, blocks, and struggles, as is, and commit to a resolution that gels with our values and goals. Ignoring, suppressing, or dismissing adversities does not lead to successful outcomes. In fact, doing so affects you in other ways you would not expect. We must avoid drifting to a scarcity mindset—believing we are incomplete and lack the tools to overcome overwhelming challenges, create infinite possibilities, and execute intentional actions.

Affirmations are concise but powerful positive statements that we consciously and subconsciously connect with to replace limiting beliefs. They inspire us to change how we think and behave and help us remain in alignment with our values and goals. The concept of affirmations mirrors the notion of "fake it till you make it," which suggests emulating or patterning a behavior that reflects the change you want to see until it becomes your reality. The more we engage with affirmations, the more the subconscious mind believes the affirmations as factual.

Affirmations have positive emotional conviction and written or spoken in the present tense. We compose affirmations to encourage powerful emotions and smother fear and doubt. Nothing worth while happens without emotion. Affirmations help us declare what we want as if we have already achieved our affirmed desire. If you set an intention to be an honest person, an example of affirmation may be "I am honest in every situation" or "I am an honest person." Notice the affirmation does not say, "I want to be honest in every situation" or "I want to be an honest person." Using the word *want* reinforces the preexisting belief that you are less than honest. The word *want* subconsciously supports the limiting belief that being honest is a challenge for you.

Changing mindset and outcomes does not need to be any more complicated than it has to be. Live and think in the present and feel the emotion that accompanies the change you would like to see.

Affirmations apply to changing attitudes, establishing a routine, and striving towards aspirations. Affirmation examples are:

- I am full of happiness, joy, and peace.
- I have everything I need to be successful.
- I visualize my goals daily.
- I eat healthily and make fitness a priority.
- I am decisive and optimistic.
- I am in control of my feelings.
- I accomplish everything I set out to do.
- I am intelligent and know where to find the answers.
- I practice active listening by being present.
- I treat everyone with the love and respect they deserve.

As you consider affirmations meaningful to you, identify beliefs and goals that make you feel good and want to commit to making the affirmation accurate.

Write your affirmations. This exercise is impactful with a few affirmations that you can read and recite with positive emotion repeatedly. Whether it's a goal, intention, or affirmation, writing a thought materializes its existence and increases the probability of success.

The subconscious mind is a long-term repository of formed habits and behaviors based on ingrained beliefs. Do not expect a subconscious metamorphosis to occur on some preset timetable. Incorporate affirmations into your daily routines until the affirmations become a natural part of your lifestyle, like brushing your teeth. As positivity and emotion saturate your subconscious mind, you will notice everything about your daily life seems and feels better. We become better individuals by cleansing and maintaining from within. Cleanse your energy, cleanse your mind, cleanse your life.

3. Surround yourself with people and ideas that align with your values and goals.

Our personal, work and geographic communities reflect our beliefs and thoughts. A dishonest person subconsciously invites dishonesty from their community into their life. A miserable person subconsciously invite misery into their life. You are the creator of your perceived reality and control the influences on your subconscious mind. Intentionally selecting your communities allows you to minimize unintended subconscious consequences and amplify intended thoughts and behaviors. We cannot determine whether our communities or certain people's quality brings us down or elevates us if we do not have a strong connection with our values.

Expanding the subconscious mind begins with taking inventory and committing to your values.

Examples of values are:

- courage
- recognition
- loyalty
- dependability
- environmentalism
- kindness

What are your values? Take this moment to write down your values. If dependability is a value, are you dependable? Are the people in your life dependable? If you are the only one in your personal community you perceive as dependable, *how* dependable are you? Perhaps you're more dependable than your friends but less dependable than you would like to be. Sometimes our expectations for others are more significant than the expectations for ourselves. If you expect people in your life to be dependable, be dependable. If you expect people in your life to be on time, exhibit timeliness. Our thoughts and behaviors should reflect our values.

Your communities should align with your values to achieve balance, fulfillment, and happiness and minimize harmful disruptions. Personal boundaries emerge when you commit to and project your values. If you feel constrained to be who you are, perhaps you should join a community that reflects and encourages your values. When you project your values and expect others to respect your values, people either work on being aligned with like values or fade from your life. If being kind is a value, and you are kind to others, relationships with those who are not kind dissolve, and relationships with those centered on kindness will flourish.

Be the person you would like the people in your life to be to you. Surround yourself with people who have similar goals and visions to minimize doubt and encourage your commitment and confidence to grow. Dreamers and optimists limit growth and success when their communities include closed-minded or pessimistic individuals.

Reprogramming the subconscious mind is a powerful concept that takes time, repetition, and consistency to be successful. Many of us have attempted change with minimal success after a life event, breakup, disappointment, or having thoughts of wanting more. When we say, "I want to change" or "I have changed," the change is more than likely temporary. Most of us attempt to fix problems we see through our perceptions but are they the *real* problem? A person may say, "I am going to finish everything I begin"—but eventually revert to the old behavior. Self-sabotaging behavior resurfaces when subconscious flaws remain or the new behavior is not consistent. Resources, such as self-help books or videos or visiting with a third party, such as a professional coach or supportive therapist, can help you address self-sabotaging behavior.

Sustainable positive change can be near impossible without a high level of self-awareness and forming subconscious habits and behaviors that support growth. So, how long does it take to reprogram the subconscious mind? It depends on your mindset and level of commitment to the work necessary to get where you want to be.

For example, the typical US military basic training program lasts seven to twelve weeks. The program's underlying purpose is to replace subconscious limiting beliefs and instill habits and behaviors to meet the military's needs. Some recruits graduate from the basic training programs, and others do not. Recruits graduate when their mental and physical commitment, trust in the process, and motivation align with their military goals.

Basic training programs take seven to twelve weeks to reprogram a military recruit's subconscious mind in a controlled environment for twenty-four hours a day. How long will it take you to reprogram your subconscious mind? The answer is in the practices and habits you adopt and your level of commitment to achieve growth. Allocating minutes a day to reprogram the subconscious mind may take a long time for characterizing changes in beliefs, thoughts, and actions to occur permanently. A general rule of thumb is an action or behavior takes over twenty days to form a habit and ninety days to become a natural part of your lifestyle. The proof is not necessarily in quantity but in the quality and consistency of reprogramming practices.

Emotion, focus, and thought are necessary to reprogram the subconscious mind. Two violinists could be equal in talent and skill and practice for the same time. One violinist may achieve the first-chair status based on his technical perfection level, while the other violinist blends in with the violin section. The first-chair violinist in this example succeeds and leads because he didn't just practice the music on the sheet—he emotionally felt each note, managed breath, and flow, and moved his limbs with grace to achieve artistic mastery.

Self-awareness and reprogramming practices must become part of your lifestyle to impact the subconscious mind. Replacing subconscious beliefs is not a task on a check list or a set-it-and-forget-it type of activity. Correcting limiting beliefs and self-sabotaging behaviors is difficult since they have become part of your neuro composition long ago. The design of our brains is for survival (fight or flight and supports a natural negative bias. We are more responsive to negativity than positivity. This simple and often unknown notion helps us understand why we resort to criticism or judgment more often than praise and anchor our thoughts to our weaknesses more than our strengths. Reprogramming the subconscious mind to overcome negative biases can be quite a feat, but you are whole and have the creativity to accomplish anything.

A great deal of positive emotion is necessary to offset our natural melancholic temperament. Positive feelings, beliefs, thoughts, and behaviors support subconscious growth. Become okay with uncertainty and acknowledge that your efforts toward change are working as your perception changes. Filter what you mentally consume to drown out instinctual negativity. Most news programming is negative because negative news sells and appeals to our negatively biased minds. Minimize information that influences negative emotions and thoughts and maximize the information you consume that supports your values and beliefs.

Practice positive self-talk. Adopt a glass-half-full instead of a half-empty perspective as your outlook on life evolves. See challenges as windows of opportunity instead of roadblocks. Focus on what you want and not what you don't want. I know this is easier said than done, but a positive mindset unblocks mental limitations that stand between you and what you want. View problems as gateways for growth. You have the power to make your rowing crew row faster and farther and move with precision to arrive at your goal destination with grace and happiness.

TIME FOR REFLECTION

An example of when I've achieved a goal but found the success limited is:

I want to become:

My intentions are:

My affirmations are:

My values are:

CHAPTER THREE

You Are Not the Boss of Me

> *"The ego is the single biggest obstruction to the achievement of anything."*
> —Richard Rose

THE SPORT OF golf—and yes, I said *sport*—is a game that is more mental than physical. The first time we swing the driver club (the longest club in the bag) to hit a golf ball, we immediately realize that a golf swing is much harder than it looks! As beginners, chances are when we swing a golf club to hit a ball, the ball flies to the right or left, or we completely miss the ball. The outcome can embarrass us if we see ourselves as capable individuals.

There is a mindful sequence of feeling, thought, and action that takes place as a golfer steps up to the ball, places the club behind the ball, coils around like a spring to bring the club back beyond the shoulder, and unwinds to swing straight through the ball. All it takes is a golf swing that sends the ball screaming down the middle of a golf course to have us coming back for more. Dad once said that he could *never* comprehend how hitting a little white ball, then chasing it toward a hole over and over could excite any player or spectator. Never say never! He is now an avid golfer and a raving fan of the sport. Funny how life works. As they say, don't knock it until you try it!

Dad and I picked up golf as he entered retirement, and I completed my finance studies. It didn't take long to realize that rounds of golf are independent of each other. It doesn't matter how well we played during the last round—there is no bearing on how well we will play in the next round. We practice in between rounds and prepare ourselves mentally and physically for a great game.

Dad and I are competitors to the core, but we have discovered that our greatest competitors are ourselves. Golf is like an ego-neutralizer; we believe that we have the game all figured out until the next round reminds us that there is more work to do.

As I step onto the golf course, my ego tells me I practiced two days ago and deserve to play well. Thoughts of the perfect swing enter my mind as I step behind the ball and stare down the wide track of green grass. My eyes are laser-focused on the back of the ball as I set the intention to launch the ball as close as possible to the hole. I begin to take the club back and forth repeatedly for practice, feeling warmed up and ready. Then I reposition myself and gently place the club adjacent to the ball. Self-doubt emerges. I begin to make adjustments to my grip, stance, and posture. After steadying myself, I swing the club back, coil with the hips and uncoil forward towards the target, powerfully guiding the club back down through the ball. At this moment, I am positive this swing is my best! Then I connect the club with the ball, and the ball launches steeply into the air, takes a hard right out of bounds, and floats down into the woods. I give myself internal parental scolding and retreat to the golf cart while mentally replaying the swing.

Golf can be a humbling experience for any of us with an overactive or unbalanced ego.

According to Sigmund Freud, the respected Austrian neurologist, ego defines personality and hinders our instincts. A balanced or neutralized ego stabilizes the subconscious and conscious states of ego that seek instant pleasure for our impulses (id) and keep us accountable to our internal rules (superego). States of the ego craft our self-image, determine our personalities and shape our behavior. Self-importance and self-doubt come from ego and can be an overcompensation for suppressed subconscious limitations. For example, some of us define ourselves by possessions and project lavish lifestyles to be admired, meet self-imposed expectations or provide a mirage of success. A luxurious lifestyle beyond financial means reflects self-sabotaging behavior driven by insecurities.

From the outside looking in, the internal voids of ourselves and others may not be blatantly obvious. Are there insecurities that feed your ego? Flawed beliefs can create a false sense of self and negatively impact our perceived reality. We may identify ourselves with being confident but project self-importance or even self-doubt. Do you defend questionable decisions or actions? Do you accept constructive feedback? Do others see you as you see yourself?

The ego can prevent us from being who we intend to be. Ego regulates thoughts and behavior, works by reason, believes in right and wrong, and fights to survive and protect us. Ego is the voice in our heads that essentially gives advice, such as "lower the golf club" or "loosen the grip" during a golf swing. Advice from an unbalanced ego contributes to irrational decisions and behavior and promotes overconfidence, fear, and doubt. Not all advice from ego is terrible. Advice from a balanced or neutralized ego sourced from subconscious beliefs of selflessness or abundance influences rational decisions and behavior.

Let's return to golf and suppose that the golf club was at the perfect height, and my grip was just right as I initially prepared to hit the ball. If this is true, then fear and doubt as presented by ego led to the adjustments that negatively impacted my golf swing. Have you ever adjusted something and then realized the outcome would have been better without the adjustment?

Negative self-talk, overconfidence, fear, and doubt create limitations and force unfavorable outcomes. Listening to and acting on misaligned advice from the ego can make us victims of our perceived reality. The quality and validity of the ego's information determine the quality of our thoughts and actions. If a flawed sense of self governs our actions, then we limit our capabilities and resourcefulness to succeed. Simple concept, but often overlooked when we are living in our heads. It was Charles R. Swindoll who said: "Life is 10 percent what happens to you and 90 percent how you react to it."

Sound familiar? Have you reacted with self-importance or self-doubt and realized later there was a better way? Have you lashed out or attacked others with little regard for the impact? Would you react the same way if you had created space between the offense and reaction? We can empower ourselves to create space and respond, not react, to situations or people by neutralizing self-importance and self-doubt. Reacting is an emotional response supported by shame, fear, anger, frustration, biases, and ego-limiting advice. We have little concern for the solution and more interest in winning or living up to unrealistic expectations. Responding is rationally considering the outcome that best aligns with our values supported by a neutralized ego. A neutralized ego occurs when self-importance and self-doubt are in balance, and we minimize destructive impulses.

An unbalanced ego urges actions and behaviors that are contradictory to our values. Meeting ourselves where we are and evaluating our beliefs and thoughts through self-awareness is how we address ego. Are you ready to look at who you are? Ego tells us we are undeserving, unworthy, and incapable or gives us an unwarranted grandiose sense of value, conceit, and pride.

We must be just as curious, if not more so, about ourselves as we are curious about others. Reprogramming the subconscious mind to replace limiting beliefs reduces the urge to act on flawed advice from the ego irrationally.

To neutralize ego, we must align our beliefs, thoughts, and actions with our values. Achieving alignment with our values shifts us from being the judges and victims of our perceived reality to being creators with empowering beliefs and controlling our emotions, thoughts, and actions.

Where are you now on your growth journey? You are reading this book. Congratulations! You want more. Wonderful! You know there is more for you. Amazing! Be grateful, not bitter, for the experiences that have brought you to this moment of wanting change for yourself.

We learned a chapter ago that there are several ways to replace limiting beliefs in the subconscious mind. Let us focus on gaining stability and control of our reality by balancing self-importance and self-doubt. Empowering and expansive views that feed ego can enable us to experience joy, happiness, peace, and success.

ADDRESSING EGO

Scottish poet Alexander Smith once said, "If the egotist is weak, his egotism is worthless. If the egotist is strong, acute, full of distinctive character, his egotism is precious and remains a possession of the race." Your ego is not bad. It has positive values; these exercises will help you find those traits.

1. Know what you cannot control and neutralize ego.

We want to believe that we can control others or outcomes, but we can only control how we react. We cannot make people feel, think, believe, or act how we would like. A flawed belief that feeds the ego—such as thinking we have control of externalities—leads to unnecessary shame, anger, stress, worry, and disappointment.

Understanding the force behind our thoughts and actions allows us to make better decisions. Are we angry or abusive to hide insecurities? Do we overcompensate for our shortcomings or what we lack?

Neutralizing ego allows you to discover your confidence in its purest form—confidence to be who you are as intended and not the image or narrative you have created for yourself and others. We learned to win, but at what price? Winning occurs by taking advantage of opportunities to learn. If we uphold a false self-image of winning, when are we evolving to become better for ourselves and others?

Internal and external struggles arise when ego dominates our thoughts and actions as we attempt to project a constant winning image of ourselves. Neutralizing ego requires acknowledging our flaws, fears, and doubts. It doesn't have to be you against the world. We all have the same inner struggles. How we deal with adversity is what sets us apart. Having neutralized ego fosters peace and confidence and minimizes conflict and strife. You are here to open doors to invite more excellent outcomes into your life and thrive as your authentic self.

2. Give yourself space to respond.

Thoughts and advice from the ego can saturate our minds, which solidifies adverse outcomes in our perceived reality. An unbalanced ego should not overpower decisions and actions. External forces should not coerce our choices and actions. Philosopher Corliss Lamont said it best: "True freedom is the capacity for acting according to one's true character, to be altogether one's self, to be self-determined and not subject to outside coercion."

Tuning into your thoughts and being vulnerable creates space to evaluate the advice of ego. Creating space or stepping back means mentally disconnecting from the situation or person to qualify your feelings and thoughts based on your values to make the best decisions and take the best actions. More times than not, we discover the best action is no action. Affirmations can be go-to mantras to check yourself. Affirmation statements such as:

- I am responsible for my decisions and actions.
- I make sound decisions and act rationally.
- I respond instead of reacting.
- I let go of what I cannot control.
- I am open to understanding the views of others.

If we react to anything from fear, a false sense of self, or selfishness, our decisions and actions are not rational and will negatively affect the outcome. Have you ever wanted to reply aggressively to an email but took a moment to switch tasks or go for a walk? Chances are the tone and choice of words in your delayed response differed from an immediate reply. Stepping back from a situation or person and observing the ego's advice introduces the opportunity for objectivity and a neutral response. Create space by pausing, reflecting, and determining whether your thoughts align with your values before taking action, providing an opportunity for an optimal resolution. If we do not create space, our emotions and thoughts may trigger a unintended reaction.

Allow your whole self to be present when connecting with your feelings, thoughts, and actions. Project precisely who you are and not who you want others to see. Align your thoughts and actions with your values to create room for understanding. Unleashing who you are with an intentional success mindset allows you to respond appropriately instead of being concerned with who wins or is right. Success is in finding and delivering the solution.

3. Listen emotionally and mentally through journaling.
Negative emotions and thoughts can fester as situations unfold and prompt an adverse reaction. A journal is a tool that can provide an outlet to redirect negativity and a point of reflection that prompts self-awareness and thought. Journal entries should begin with the entry date, expressions of gratitude and end with affirmations. Scribe each entry as if you're in the situation's moment, but with an open mind. Pause every so often to gauge your feelings and thoughts. Is the limiting advice of ego as present as before? Does the situation seem as frustrating as it did initially? As you review your entry, you may find the problem less meaningful or emotional or that the best response is now clear.

When you have positive experiences and responses to situations, record them in your journal as well. How did you feel responding from a place of selflessness and love? Reflect on the experience in terms of your feelings and thoughts. How did responding in control of your feelings and thoughts differ from situations where you reacted?

Reflect on your emotions and thoughts before, during, and after journaling to broaden your perceived reality and engage your resourcefulness to resolve situations favorably. How difficult is it for outside forces to rattle you or draw unbecoming behavior from you? The answers in life are not clear when the haze of an unbalanced ego is present.

4. Establish an accountability partner.
An accountability partner can be a third-party that may be going through a similar transformation and can hold you accountable to your goal of neutralizing ego. They can ask additional questions to prompt reflection from a varying perspective. By having an accountability partner, we can avoid thinking we have all the answers, or uncover responses we haven't considered.

If the ego is our judge and the judge is biased or we view ourselves as victims, fear, self-importance, entitlement, and a false sense of self affect confidence in our responses. Our actions may be loftier than they should. An accountability partner is not an advisor but a sounding board to share perspective. The partner may ask questions such as, "What options do you think may lead to a successful solution?"or "Which approach do you feel may lead to the best outcome?" Be mindful in selecting your accountability partner.

Select an accountability partner who:

1. exhibits objectivity and not attached to the situation itself or the outcome of the partnership;
2. has your best interest in mind and inspires you to be a better person; and
3. is further along on their growth journey.

Situations present opportunities to realign our intentions. Many of us mishandle opportunities by reacting instead of responding based on our values. Responding with inner peace gives us power and strength over limiting emotions, thoughts, and actions. We become egotistically healthier and position ourselves to progress toward positive outcomes with balanced opinions, thoughts, and actions.

Are your thoughts coming from peace or fear? Changing the quality of our thoughts neutralizes ego. Ego can be selective in deciding the advice we receive, so it's essential to assess the advice to achieve balance.

TIME FOR REFLECTION

My ego has affected my goals by:

I intend to start responding, not reacting, by:

My affirmations are:

I intend to get a journal by the following date:

My accountability partner is:

To me, a neutralized ego is:

To me, an unbalanced ego is:

CHAPTER FOUR

But Did You Die?

"I never lose. I either win or learn."
—Nelson Mandela

THE FIRST TIME a girl broke up with me occurred in a relationship we often referred to as a romantic comedy or rom-com. Everything we did, and I do mean *everything*, resulted in pure comedy and romance. If our relationship were a movie, it would have been a box office hit! We shared laughs and experiences, communicated with compassion, complimented each other daily, and prioritized each other's goals and ambitions. It was the type of relationship that made couples question the fire and validity of their relationship. It was the type of love that made strangers approach us and comment on the vibrant energy felt by being near us.

Welp, the relationship crashed and burned just as fast as it passionately blossomed. Fast love does not necessarily mean long love, my friends. The breakup itself was minor, but the piercing thorn in my side was that I wanted her back.

Let's pause here and note the thought of *want*. *Want* comes from a place of lack. What did I lack?

I chased my ex like how men in rom-coms pursue the loves of their lives! You know, the scene in every romance movie where a love-struck man rushes through the most crowded airport to stop his woman from boarding the plane. Or the man who sprints across the city park to stop his lady and the most raggedy moving truck from leaving the city with her three pieces of furniture. We've all seen the movie scene, just before the credits, where the man uses perfect words to get his woman back, and they live happily ever after, right?

Chasing anyone in the name of love only works in the movies. If we're chasing someone, it means they are running from us. After failing to rekindle a relationship that died like the sole remaining leaf during the last stages of fall, I paused and reflected on the situation. I could either let this situation scar me for life or be grateful for the experience and create a reality of abundance. When we feel lost or have feelings of lack, we must recenter ourselves by taking inventory of what we do have and expressing gratitude. Gratitude replaces feelings of lack with abundance.

The overdue self-healing journey began by letting go of the hope that there would be a rom-com part two. I let go of judgment, blame, guilt, and disappointment and accepted that we both did the best we could when we were together. As a competitive person who had sought triumph, I had to win by learning and detaching from the experience. A happy and fulfilled life is about balance. We are humble, or we will be humbled and humbled I was.

To return whole, I recommitted to my values and reunited with my purpose. I gave myself space to grieve and reconnect with friends and family. We need reminders of unconditional love and care after a breakup. Friends and family can be glorious reminders. I avoided attracting another girlfriend and worked on myself. I loved on me like I wanted others to love me. I did things for myself that others did for me and much more. Over time, I lacked nothing, and my mindset was one of abundance. Everything my ex had provided me through our relationship, I could provide for myself. Day by day, week by week, as I focused on myself, self-respect grew, clear boundaries formed, and self-confidence erupted. I bounced back, but better than ever! My interests evolved, and outlook changed. Instead of being bitter about the breakup, I became grateful for the experience.

Change your mindset, change your results.

A self-healing journey for any of us is the epitome of death and rebirth. We don't die, but our attachment to the experience dies. By letting go, I created a new reality filled with happiness, joy, and peace. I felt, behaved, and glowed differently. Relationships that were not in alignment with my values and goals effortlessly dissolved. Relationships that matched my values grew more robust, and new meaningful relationships formed. My trust in the letting-go process had erected a foundation for limitless growth, happiness, and success like never before. All we have to do is let go, change our mindset, trust the process, and we can rise above anything!

The concept of letting go means different things to different people. Many of us do not know how to let go. Let go and let God, right? People tell us to let go, but what does it mean to let go?

- Letting go is having self-awareness and accepting what is not for us.
- Letting go is detaching emotions, thoughts, and actions from the experience.
- Letting go is completely releasing what we cannot control.
- Letting go is self-healing by redirecting focus to our values.

Letting go is straightforward, but in reality, it's challenging depending on where we are on our growth journey. We know we should let go but instead force our will on the situation or outcome, building up disappointment. Letting go of what no longer serves us unblocks abundance and allows us to receive what is for us.

Our struggles with letting go begin by holding on to the past, hoping, or believing we can control or manipulate an outcome in our favor. Aligning our emotions, thoughts, and actions with our values allows us to move past what *was* to what *is*.

What does letting go of experiences and outcomes mean to you? Do you know when to let go? How have you struggled with letting go? What has to occur for you to let go?

I don't know what you need to let go, but most of us need help to let go of regret or something that we feel defeated us. Maybe for you, letting go applies to:

- Marriage
- Career
- School
- Finances
- Health

Prayers and manifestations cannot respond to your request until we have let go of the outcome. Having faith in the process encourages reflection and growth and allows us to move from a mindset of lack to abundance. Successfully letting go is possible by focusing on the present and relinquishing the attachment to the experience or what did and didn't occur.

LETTING GO

It took time, but I let go of the rom-com relationship. I stopped chasing and progressively healed. Allow me to guide you to leaving the past in the past and intentionally focus on the present. As you read these steps, think about lingering hurts or current setbacks you need to leave behind.

1. Redirect focus to you.

When we attach to someone or something, the most challenging task is to shift focus to ourselves. How do you shift focus to yourself? Do you have conflicting feelings and thoughts about letting go? Maybe you want to let go but don't want to lose sight of the experience or even hope. If letting go means overcoming a loss, we need to feel the loss and grieve organically, step-by-step, to become healed. Suffering with the intention of healing leads to acceptance and encourages growth. Acceptance moves us forward without the past dictating our emotions, thoughts, or actions.

Forgive yourself by genuinely believing that you did everything you could and that everything occurred as intended. Focusing inward to gain awareness of your emotions and thoughts helps you create emotional space to heal. Avoid fixating on the experience by discarding or putting away visual reminders, such as photos or anything that reminds you of the person or thing. Visuals trigger emotion and thought. Letting go leads to change by dissolving regrets of the past and fear of the future. Fall in love with you by getting to know you from the inside out! If there are activities you enjoy, do them. Workout, go camping, or travel. If you enjoy spending time with friends and family, spend time with friends and family. Make yourself a priority by providing yourself the love you have to give others. Be as grateful for the experience as you are for the healing process.

Our emotions and thoughts can attach us to the past and keep us latched onto what we want or lack. Have trust in your ability to let go. It takes a monumental effort to let go, but you can do it. Meet yourself where you are and acknowledge that you have everything you need and want within you. Only then can you heal and grow.

2. Visualize.

Imagery shapes our perceived reality. If we visualize ourselves as healed, we will gain confidence in the healing process and heal.

Since the subconscious mind does not know the difference between "real life" and imagination, we have healed. Over time, lack and the attachment dissolves, and our positive emotions can create thoughts and actions that invite better outcomes.

Visualizing and believing in positive outcomes invites what we desire into our lives. If you're suffering from heartbreak, see yourself as a happy person and doing things you enjoy. Visualize living out your purpose and contributing to the lives of others. See yourself feeling peace as you surround yourself with people who sincerely care and treat you in alignment with your values. What makes you feel good or fulfilled? Where do you redirect the emotions and thoughts when letting go of the past?

Many of us redirect our emotions and thoughts to our passions or whatever sparks the feeling of abundance. Seeing yourself as healed and living life as if you have already moved on propels you forward toward being whole. We can let go of anyone or anything that is unhealthy for us.

3. Trust the process.

We experience any level of success when we have an effective combination of emotions, thoughts, actions, and most importantly, patience. Letting go requires patience to achieve peace. We often look for instant gratification once we glimpse progress and surrender our efforts or abort the game plan prematurely. Knowing and understanding how to let go is just the start.

The proof that you are healing comes when you wholeheartedly apply the letting go process and believe without a doubt that you are better off detached from the past. Negative emotions and thoughts embedded with doubt, fear, worry, and frustration surface from time to time, but that's okay. The horizon may look bleak, but we must know sunshine is on its way. How you deal with unwanted thoughts and emotions is all that matters. If you try to avoid or suppress negative feelings and thoughts, the dominance of their presence becomes more significant, halting or delaying the process.

So, what can you do to reclaim your mind? Observe the thoughts and feel the emotions, then move on by embracing and engaging the present moment. Focus on the present moment by immersing yourself in the atmosphere and task at hand. If you're taking a shower, feel the beads of water caressing your skin and saturate your thoughts with the intimate process of taking a shower. If you're with your kids, engage with them with all of your emotions and thoughts. Be with them much more than physically. The mind can only consider one thought at a time so that you can redirect energy and emotion. By prioritizing the immediate present with positivity and gratitude, nothing else can mindfully exist.

When we do not let go, negative emotions or thoughts limit our potential to heal and receive. Suppressing feelings leaves unresolved baggage that reclaim us down the road. Let it go and be free for new experiences.

Have you listened to a story, and as the person shared the story, they emotionally relived the experience with every word? News flash! They haven't let go. We may also know people who ruin relationships with self-sabotaging behavior. People do not intentionally screw up relationships, but if they haven't let go or healed from their past, they are limiting the potential of all relationships going forward. Letting go creates space for internal reconciliation and opens the door for higher levels of fulfillment and happiness.

Lingering limiting beliefs from attachments live in the subconscious mind. The beliefs become entrenched in our perceived reality and stifle our ability to grow and move forward. We essentially become paralyzed without realizing it and tie ourselves to subconscious baggage. A butterfly can't fly while clinging onto the cocoon. Spread your wings and let go. Repressed emotions and thoughts can unknowingly emerge, affecting decisions and actions in the present.

Our past can lead us to:

- judge ourselves or others unfairly;
- attack to protect ourselves;
- live our lives as victims;
- worry about what we cannot control; and
- exhibit unhealthy behaviors that limit happiness and success.

We may think we are making decisions as information arrives, but our flawed beliefs can taint our thoughts and actions if we haven't let go. Let go gracefully, experience unblocked abundance, and allow greater happiness and success into your life.

TIME FOR REFLECTION

People and things I should let go:

I am grateful for:

I forgive myself for:

What does it mean to be healed:

I enjoy:

I love:

CHAPTER FIVE

Feel the Vibration

"Everything is energy. Match the frequency of the reality you want and you cannot help but get that reality. It can be no other way. This is not philosophy. This is physics."
—Albert Einstein

As CHILDREN, MY friends and I were our happiest when playing outdoors. We could not get enough of the fun that awaited us as we exited our homes once receiving the seal of approval from our protectors. We enjoyed the outdoors from sunrise until the streetlights come on just before dusk. We would return home during the day only to check-in or for refreshments. The concept of time seemed so obscure. Outside meant freedom and adventure and learning to work through whatever came our way. A fall on the pavement was a minor disruption. Tussles with the neighborhood kids were temporary blemishes on the day. We lived in the now and gave little thought to yesterday or tomorrow. Our feelings and thoughts were always positively fueled with energy and endless curiosity about life.

What happens to our childhood joy and curiosity as we become adults? It's as if we transition from having happy-go-lucky thoughts about life to being stressful and worrisome. We find it takes effort to achieve and maintain higher energy levels as we take on responsibilities and obligations. We become victims of routine and lose sight of the simple things that made us smile or reenergized us as children.

As with anything in life, no matter what we go through or what comes our way, we can be in complete control of ourselves and happiness. We are still the children who were once excited about spending all day on the playground. The only difference is, as adults, our playgrounds are different.

Hiking trails and golf courses have become my playgrounds of choice. As I head out to hike or play golf, I am as excited as a six-year-old lad heading out to play in the backyard with his closest pals. For hiking, in particular, I pack gear and snacks for a four-mile hike as if I plan to be in the wild for a week. Don't judge me. You never know! The good vibes that come with being mindfully outdoors by listening to nature and navigating rocks and tree roots re-introduce feelings of happiness, joy, and peace that were present as a kid. A good hike provides an opportunity to elevate vibrational energy, be mindful, and return with emotional and mental clarity. Do you have a playground that creates emotional and mental space for you?

To understand the concepts of vibrational energy, let's go back to school for a moment. The universe, everything we can touch and feel, consists of energy, including ourselves. Energy transforms, converts, and transfers into other forms. Under an electron microscope, energy appears as molecules that vibrate at varying speeds. The brain sends signals as transformed energy to our muscles to stimulate movement and coordination. The mind—a result from brain activity, creates awareness of our presence, experiences, feelings, and thoughts through converted energy. Energy transfers from the brain to the mind, to the body; it is inseparable. Self-awareness is energy transformed or converted that consciously enables us to observe feelings, thoughts and evaluate experiences intentionally. Vibrational energy handles all that we are and the reality we create. Our feelings, beliefs, thoughts, and actions that contribute to who we are, are all forms of transformed or converted energy. Thus, vibrational energy affects our whole being. As Einstein said, "This is not philosophy. This is physics."

All of us have felt vibrational energy or vibrations from someone. Being aware of vibrational energy can help us understand how our vibrational energy can impact our perceived reality and closest communities. The vibrational energy or frequency rate varies based on whether our energy centers on positivity or negativity. High vibrational frequencies associate with higher consciousness levels that closely align with love, joy, and peace and support positive behaviors and outcomes. Lower vibrational frequencies associate with lower levels of consciousness, such as fear, guilt, and shame, and support negative behaviors and outcomes. Higher vibrations make us feel light, while lower vibrations make us feel emotionally, mentally, and even physically heavy.

Let's consider how the presence of a perky morning person can light up a room without saying a word. Morning people exhibit high vibrational energy and radiate from upper levels of consciousness as they start their day. The presence of morning people may help many of us elevate our vibrations, while others may choose to distance ourselves since our vibrations do not match. Without coffee, some of us operate from lower frequencies, sparking discomfort or jealously when around morning people. Does this sound like you?

Our energy should match what we intend to invite into our lives. If we want to invite love, our vibrational frequency, elevated by the love we provide ourselves, should match the love we desire. Like attracts like. Once we know the impact that vibrational energy has on perceived reality, we can use vibrational energy, effectively, and efficiently to live life as we choose.

Dr. David R. Hawkins, a renowned psychiatrist and spiritual teacher, has conducted studies using an algorithmic energy frequency scale and consciousness levels to determine individuals' behavior. Dr. Hawkins concluded that over 75 percent of the world's population operates at lower consciousness levels.[1] Let that sink in for a moment. Dr. Hawkins's conclusions make sense if we recall our brains have a negative bias. Think about how much stress, anger, worry, fear, depression, and anxiety there is in the world. Imagine what the world would be like if more people had elevated levels of vibrational energy and experienced feelings, thoughts, and actions associated with higher consciousness levels. The world as we know it would be a much better place!

Positive thoughts, emotions, and actions raise vibrational frequencies and invite positive outcomes. We cannot control the world, but we can increase our vibrational frequencies to change our perceived reality and impact our communities positively. Changing our perceived reality may not seem like it can influence the world on the surface, but all it takes is one person to impact the world. We can influence our communities with positive vibes and intentional actions that affect the people we connect with.

Let's consider the concept of paying it forward. We'll review a time when patrons in the vehicle ahead in the fast-food drive-through line purchased our order for us. The gesture made us feel wonderful and we expressed gratitude, elevating our vibrational frequencies.

The remainder of the day seemed better than expected. We felt compelled to do something special for someone else, making us feel even better. Now that person is grateful, uplifted, and will do something kind for someone else. The compounding effect of higher vibrations is infinite and begins with evolving our perceived reality. The energy that I put into writing this book is transferring to you as you read and feel inspired by each message. Your vibrational energy is increasing as you change your perceived

1 Dr. David R. Hawkins, *Transcending the Levels of Consciousness: The Stairway to Enlightenment* (Carlsbad, CA: Hay House UK).

reality and positively affect those in your communities. Each of us can be resourceful and creative to make a difference in ourselves that positively impacts others.

Successfully raising our vibrational frequencies to higher levels and closely aligning our actions with our intentions allows us to feel and believe that everything in our lives is happening in our favor. We know this euphoric feeling as being in the zone, flow, or a flow state. In the zone, we are thriving in the present and immersing ourselves in our day and activities. We have a confident sense of self, feel happy, loved, and experience a lightness as if all concerns about the past and fears of the future have vanished. All of our interactions seem positive and effortless. We instinctively want to share our story and help others so they, too, can feel the vibes that we are experiencing. Stating a simple, joyful greeting such as "Good morning!" has more meaning for you than the receiver. Physical pain or uncomfortable tenderness, if any, may feel less or minimal. Mental focus and clarity come with ease. Daily tasks are more enjoyable, and everything we do with intention seems to lead to a successful outcome. We transfer positive energy, invite positive outcomes, and feel abundant!

When we replace negativity with positivity, we can expand our awareness and increase our vibrations. Our lives can change significantly by leveling up the quality of vibrations to drive positive thoughts and actions.

Understanding vibrational energy empowers us to create a perceived reality that invites what we desire and intentionally opens the doorway for favorable outcomes. Raising vibrational energy promotes the emotions primed for positive and actionable impact. If we want to live an intentional life centered on peace, love, and joy, we must raise our vibrations and project higher consciousness levels to invite peace, love, and joy. It is that simple. Simplicity depends on our present level of consciousness and how effectively we can create space. We can't fool the universe. Thinking but not believing positively limits positive emotion and action. Some people say positive things but display negative or contradictory actions. That's unhealthy. Achieving higher vibrational energy starts with the intentional will to believe, think, and behave according to our values, goals, and desires. Regardless of where we are presently in terms of mindset, we can expand our conscious awareness and raise our vibration to create a reality greater than imagined.

RAISING YOUR VIBRATIONAL FREQUENCY

You are energy, and you transfer energy. All energy is not favorable. Ensure the energy you put out into the world is good. The steps below help improve your awareness of negative vibrational energy and guide you to raise and maintain higher vibrational frequencies.

1. Love on you.

Embrace who you are and let go of negative thoughts saturated with shame, jealousy, resentment, anger, and guilt. Zero in on your strengths and focus on being happy.

When was the last time you have been to your playground for an emotional and mental reset? Perhaps you geek out by going to the gym—then do that! If you enjoy mindful meditation sessions, make time in your daily schedule.

Other playground activities may be:

- Cooking or baking
- Getting a massage
- Painting or drawing
- Dancing or singing
- Camping or hiking
- Writing or reading
- Volunteering

- Cuddling with animals
- Sewing or knitting
- Listening to music
- Gardening

Accepting and loving *you* provides a foundation to understand and transform the whole self.

Negative thoughts and lower levels of consciousness will struggle to have a place in your mind as you consistently think positively and operate at higher vibrational frequencies. You may find certain situations or people no longer have a place in your life. Commit to yourself and set nonnegotiable boundaries to elevate self-respect. If you project and value authenticity, abstain from people who are not authentic. If you project and value integrity, refrain from allowing people without integrity to disrupt your life. Everyone is not your friend or has your best interest in mind. As you align your actions with your values, people will view and interact with you differently, creating opportunities for you to raise and maintain higher vibrations.

2. Replace negative self-talk.

Negative self-talk in any way affects our feelings, thoughts, and actions. Some negative self-talk can limit how much we believe in ourselves and our abilities. If you make a mistake, learn from it and let it go. Do not criticize or beat yourself up for the misstep. What's the point? Nothing changes.

Negative self-talk misaligns your thoughts with your values and invites adverse outcomes. We invite what we think about. As you find yourself talking negatively, replace the negative thoughts with positivity. Change the self-talk. For example, if you make a mistake and typically say, "I'm so stupid" instead say, "I'm a great learner." Productive self-talk centers on positivity. Practices that support positivity do wonders for the subconscious mind with repetition. Other negative self-talk replacements and affirmations may be:

- "I focus on the solution, not the problem."
- "I have everything within me to be happy."
- "I am in control over my thoughts, actions, and behavior."
- "I am worthy of being treated with dignity and respect."
- "I am enough."

Replace negative self-talk with positive self-talk when criticizing others. Change "He knows nothing" to "He is great at finding answers." Practice and consistency in promoting positivity raise your vibrational energy and can influence the frequencies of others.

3. Filter everything you mentally consume.

I won't use this step as an opportunity to discuss conspiracy theories, but everything you hear and see may not have your best interest in mind. Plain and simple.

Monitor the information you are allowing into your mind. All information is not productive, favorable, or consciously communicated. We experience subliminal messages and virtue signaling in different forms, primarily through television. We are typically unaware of the messages that live in our subconscious mind. The constant absorption of low vibration information can contribute to our negative biases, and trigger self-sabotaging behavior.

As humans, we faithfully believe in what we can see, hear, smell, and touch. If we are unaware of how negative information is affecting us, we believe negative information does not affect our well-being.

But it does. For example, studies show that the risk of copycat suicides increases when movies contain suicidal content.[2]

As an experimental observation, stand outside the exit doors as a movie ends at a theater. If the film was lighthearted and provided a positive message, movie-goers will smile and have enjoyable conversations as they exit. If the movie has violence or a dark subject, movie-goers appear somber, non-expressive, with hands in pockets, and have simplistic discussions, if any. They are mentally processing the lingering lower frequency messages conveyed visually and audibly.

We can filter the information we consume by being selective of our sources of information. Like a diet where we watch what we eat, we should be mindful of what we mentally consume. Be your parental control with content that is not productive or does not align with your values. The more you practice filtering information, the more you support higher vibrational energy levels, and easier mental filtering becomes.

4. Eat right and exercise consistently.

I mentioned that energy will always exist and can only transfer, convert, or transform. Let us apply this simple concept to food. Higher vibrational foods have higher levels of nutritional value and are less processed. Eating low-processed foods and avoiding artificial additives enable the body to use the nutrients to support the mind and body efficiently. Water is essential to transport vibrational energy and maintain our internal functions. Consuming water delivers nutrients and discards toxins from our bodies. We think, feel, focus, and exercise better with higher vibrational foods and plenty of water.

---

2 Benedikt Till, Ulrich S. Tran, et al, "Associations between Film Preferences and Risk Factors for Suicide: An Online Survey," NCBI, published July 16, 2014, https://www.ncbi.nlm.nih.gov/pmc/articles/PMC4100813/.

Exercise raises our vibrations and supplies oxygen to the brain, creating a chain reaction of benefits—from changes in mood and body composition to increases in strength. People who exercise tend to make better food choices and drink more water. Just thirty minutes of exercise a few times a week can raise your frequencies and affect how you feel and behave.

5. Express gratitude.

We can quickly get wrapped up in what we need or don't have in today's day and age. Expressing gratitude daily raises vibrational energy and expands awareness. As you take inventory of all that you are and have in your life, express gratitude to uplift emotion and thought.

There are many ways to include gratitude expressions into your daily routine, such as using a gratitude journal where you journal everything that you are grateful for each day. Another way to express gratitude is to convey gratefulness to yourself and others verbally. Look for opportunities to incite hope, encourage others, and give thanks. Your vibrational energy will increase, and so will theirs.

Incorporate gratitude affirmations into your morning and evening routines, such as, "I am grateful to be alive and happy this morning" or "I am grateful to have had such a wonderful day." Post stickies with gratitude affirmations on your bathroom mirror to remind you of everything you are grateful for as you brush your teeth before starting your day or going to bed. Say a prayer of thanks or meditate in gratitude. If you are a visual person, create a gratitude jar to add expressions of gratitude each day. Pull from the jar from time to time to reflect on your submissions. Over time, as the jar fills, you will feel grateful and see the abundance of what you have. Gratitude and intention are at the core of everything that becomes great.

We've discussed and learned how to apply our innate vibrational energy capabilities from a science perspective. Now let's talk metaphysically for a moment.

Our inner body, or nonphysical body, has seven energy centers that begin at the base of our spines and run upward, ending at the top of our heads. The energy centers, also known as *chakras*, are whirlpools of energy and connect our inner body to our physical body. Each chakra has a circular shape and is near different body areas, such as the heart, throat, and lower abdomen. Chakras originated with Hindu and Tantra Buddhism traditions. Their purpose is to swirl in energy from our aura, the electromagnetic energy the surrounds us, to balance our spiritual, mental, emotional, and physical health. Peace comes when all chakras are open and in balance.

Many of us, may have blocked or overactive chakras. Since we cannot destroy energy, a blocked chakra causes the other chakras to be more active than if the blocked chakra was open. Blocked and overactive chakras throw off our overall health. The balance of energy between the chakras depends on each chakra's vibrational frequency. As we raise our vibrational energy, the chakras vibrate more in harmony and improve our well-being. Practices such as yoga, meditation, washing a car, and chanting can open blocked chakras and bring energy distribution in balance.

Whether we speak scientifically or metaphysically, vibrational energy is essential to our conscious awareness, perceived reality, and overall well-being. Everything in life is linked to vibrational energy. We can apply a blend of positive energy and emotions and intentional thoughts and actions to invite happiness and success into our lives. If everything in life begins with intention and energy transforms intention into outcomes, everything we want begins and ends with energy.

TIME FOR REFLECTION

My playground is:

I have high or low [circle one] vibrational energy.

I intend to raise my vibrational energy by doing the following:

My nonnegotiable boundaries are:

My negative self-talk replacements and affirmations are:

I intend to adjust what I mentally consume by:

I intend to start eating these high vibrational foods:

I intend to start exercising by:

I intend to begin using a gratitude jar, journal, or stickies by the following date:

CHAPTER SIX

Just Let Me Love You

"What lies behind us and what lies before us are tiny matters compared to what lies within us."
—Ralph Waldo Emerson

I HAVEN'T HAD the honor of being a parent, but parenting has to be the most crucial role that could exist in another human's life. Two people with differing beliefs, observations, and experiences have the opportunity to teach, direct, and encourage their offspring to be valuable contributors to society and good people. Wow, what a concept. In a single-parent household, the challenge to raise happy and successful children is even more incredible!

Parents compete with negative influences from television programming, neighborhood kids, and social media and inherent biases to place their children on track for greatness. Children do not come with instruction manuals, how-to videos, or training classes. (What could go wrong?) Depending on the parenting style, child-rearing environment, and consistency in communication, children can grow up in alignment with parental intentions or different from expectations.

Dad worked for the army by day and attended college classes by night. Mom operated a child-learning center at home by day, worked at the mall by night, and attended nursing school years later. Both provided everything I needed and wanted at will, which is different from their respective Jamaican childhoods before migrating to the US. Children can become entitled to receive, develop a scarcity mindset, and compare themselves to others. Dad was well aware of the comfortable lifestyle he provided us and determined to offer balance. Family vacations in Jamaica did not include:

- staying at an all-inclusive resort,
- playing in the hotel pool from sunrise until sundown, or
- enjoying thrill-seeking activities and excursions.

Vacations for us were in St. Catherine, one of the poorest parishes of Jamaica. Dad grew up there in a three-room (two-bedrooms) cinderblock house where he shared a queen-size bed with five siblings after his dad saved enough money to add the two bedrooms. Talk about living in close quarters. Household appliances, indoor plumbing, and grocery stores were all wishful thinking. To give his children an appreciation of the purposeful sacrifice and hard work that led to the abundant lifestyle we experienced in the US, Dad coordinated travel to Jamaica for extended visits and to get a sense of "country." Country included bathing in the river, living off the land, and making the most out of the simple things.

Just before the age of seven, I joined Dad on a trip to Jamaica. I was so excited as we landed, not only because it was just Dad and me but also because I enjoyed roughing it! There is something about being one with nature and living to tell the story. Okay, maybe this was not a death-defying experience, but it was pretty different from the comfortable life I had at home.

We traveled from the airport and parked the rental car off a less heavily traveled dirt road to head to our living quarters for the next three weeks. To get to Dad's childhood home, we walked through a narrow mile stretch of hilly red clay terrain lined with wilderness with our belongings in tow. The path was not safe or wide enough for vehicles. There were no streetlights or tour guides, and we could barely see our hands in front of us! As visitors from "Foreign"—what Jamaicans call the US—we appear as walking treasure chests to those with malicious intent. In the pitch of dark and with no guarantees for our safety or feelings of security, I had to trust that everything would be okay, let go of negative thoughts, and hang on to Dad's instructions.

Focusing on the moment, being mindful with every step, and not fearing the sounds of nocturnal creatures was a lesson in itself. During our stay, I woke up with the roosters, indulged in national fruit and dishes, raised a goat that later became a meal, constructed a slingshot from the inner tube of a bicycle tire, and turned a vendor cart into a go-cart. All experiences there taught me something about myself and added value to the pilgrimage of becoming an adult.

Life in this part of Jamaica was minimalistic but provided the richest experiences. I did not have access to the simple luxuries back home, but I was at my happiest. I did not miss material possessions, life conveniences, or even the neighborhood kids. As I got to know the Jamaican neighbors, I began to understand what Dad had been trying to show me—to be grateful, attach to nothing but connect to everything. The locals owned a little more than the clothes on their backs but did not have a scarcity mindset. They were living in abundance, overflowing with gratitude, happiness, joy, and peace. What more do any of us need? The neighbors were grateful to be alive, live off the food that Mother Nature provided and to experience togetherness. They lived unattached to future outcomes. Work, finances, or the past were not mental burdens. No problem.

"No problem, mon" is a saying often expressed by Jamaicans and an underrated attestation of their calm and relaxed temperament. The neighbors projected love and connected to everything around them, mindfully and spiritually. Everything they needed and wanted was within reach.

I share this story with you as not only an example of how experiences can broaden perspective and expand perceived reality but as a story that illustrates the value of being whole. This trip to Jamaica has become a massive collection of defining moments that allowed me to fall in love with myself. As children, getting the next new toy, staying up an extra hour, and hearing certain classmates' words could make or break our spirits. If we are not aware of our energy, emotions, beliefs, and thoughts, we can create a perceived reality that differ from our intentions. Are you happy? What does happiness look like for you? Do you know what it takes for you to be happy? To be happy is to know oneself, share joy, and be secure from within, like the Jamaican neighbors.

Self-love is the practice of making happiness a priority spiritually, mentally, and physically. Loving yourself starts with understanding and embracing who you are, as you are, on every level. Have you said yes to things or activities that did not align with your values? Have you abandoned your needs too often for others? Do you reach for happiness externally? The people we often neglect the most are ourselves.

As we go through life, we attach to things, people, work, places, and experiences. When we attach to anything, we lose touch with our authentic selves and become less of who we are and more of who we are not. It is a zero-sum game; your loss is another's gain, but the net benefit to both is zero. Yet, we attach ourselves regularly. Our authentic self is who we are at the purest level without being attached to the picture-perfect family, fancy car, illustrious career, or big house. Who are you without attachments? Does your job define you? Are you motivated by expectations? Who are you?

Self-love positions us to embrace connections over attachments. What is the difference? When we are whole and connected, we live in the present and share our peace, joy, and happiness without losing ourselves. When attached, we need feedback, acceptance, and validation to feel whole, loved, and happy. We should not need a career promotion, a certain sum of money, or a particular relationship to be whole. Attachments are grounded in self and neediness, occurring when we externally fill an inner void. We depend on someone or something to complete some aspect of our lives. We feel like life is over without the presence of the person or thing when we are emotionally or physically attached. Sharing happiness is healthier than sharing the neediness to be happy.

For example, some of us may believe that the next house, job, or relationship will make us happy. You, and only you, are responsible for your happiness and fulfillment. A person or thing carries no responsibility for your happiness and to make you whole. When we establish intentional connections, we are happy and fulfilled regardless of the person or thing's presence. We'll grieve over a loss but survive and continue to thrive after that. Connections are emotional, centered on the mind and spirit, instead of self. Higher self-awareness enables us to experience rewarding relationships and let go of what we cannot control.

We all have heard the saying, "You have to love yourself before you can love anyone else," but do we know what the expression means? When we love ourselves, compliments or feedback are unnecessary to feel secure or complete. Loving ourselves means we do not need opinions or comparisons to make us feel worthy or loved. We also do not need to manipulate or control others to create belongingness or receive "love." Love yourself to know you are enough and invite people into your life who are secure and confident with the love they have for themselves. They don't want neediness, nor do you.

Self-love encourages us to be comfortable with ourselves and gain inner peace. Loving ourselves and being connected instead of attached removes blinders that block us from being intuitive and intentional and gives us space to respond with grace from a secure place of self-worth and positivity. If rejection comes our way, we see the occurrence as closing a path not meant for us, instead of a point of agony and despair. When someone unfairly criticizes us, we should see the criticism as a reflection of their insecurities instead of owning the criticism and questioning our worth. When we commit to our values and understand who we are, we live detached from opinions, comparisons, and expectations that are not aligned with our values and goals. The moment we realize we don't need or want anything externally to be happy, we become powerfully connected to our communities. If we are happy and whole, we will make high quality decisions and bring positivity toward ourselves. Self-love empowers us to inspire and be better people.

Happiness comes from within and allows us to create an abundant reality. Do you check in with yourself? Are you honest when someone asks you, "How are you doing?" or do you give a vague, socially acceptable response? If you do not check in with you, who will? We are in control of the realities we create. No one can care for you more than you. Okay, maybe your Mom can, but you are the only one who authentically knows how you feel.

As we return to our authentic selves through self-love, we can share more of ourselves with others without losing ourselves. We become generous and eager to share our love, peace, and positive energy and build meaningful connections. Our perceived reality receives an upgrade. We feel compelled to serve and inspire others to be whole because we have seen the value of focusing inward to achieve happiness and peace.

PRACTICING SELF-LOVE

The demands of our lifestyles pull us away from caring for ourselves and affect our wellness and happiness. Practicing self-love enables us to achieve balance to give our most incredible value to ourselves and the world at large. Add self-love as a critical component to your growth journey by becoming more in-tune with you and appreciating the one-of-a-kind person you are. With some time and consistency, you'll develop a healthy relationship with yourself that can confidently overcome limitations and challenges.

1. Forgive yourself.

We, as go-getters, are always our own worst critics. Do you harbor ill will toward yourself for past mistakes? Do you sabotage good things or relationships that enter your life? We judge or blame ourselves and feel shame or guilt for past decisions that did not work out as we expected. Forgive yourself. You deserve it! We cannot change the past, but we can thrive in the present by aligning with our values and eliminating negative self-talk.

Replace every negative thought with three positive thoughts about yourself. Every time negative thoughts surface, think of the three positive thoughts. Here are some examples to get you started:

- Change "I never do anything right" to "I can do anything I focus on."
- Change "I overthink everything" to "I consider what I can control."
- Change "This is too hard, I give up" to "I have what it takes to accomplish this."

Consider creating notes with three positive thoughts and placing them in visible places, such as on a mirror, in your car, or even the lock or home screen of your cell phone. Eventually, the negative thoughts will fade and matter less. Remember, the conscious mind can only focus on a single thought at a time, so make it a positive thought!

2. Write self-love affirmations and review often.

Self-love minimizes self-sabotaging behavior and supports the emotions and thoughts necessary for intentional actions. In your journal, write several self-love affirmations. I prefer to start my entries with "I love . . ." so the affirmations are not any less meaningful than the spoken words of love given to another individual. Start each journal entry with expressions of gratitude to prime the mind, and then move on to simple affirmation statements, such as:

- I love not apologizing for being me.
- I love that I surround myself with people who share the same values.
- I love that I genuinely care for others.
- I love who I am and what I stand for.
- I love that my happiness comes from within.

Practicing positive self-talk with the powerful emotion of love and reviewing your affirmation statements boosts self-confidence and reaffirms positive thoughts. For convenience, add your affirmation statements to your cell phone, notepad or planner to review when self-doubt or negative thoughts seep into your day.

3. Be intentional about saying yes.

Some of us feel compelled to please others by saying yes when we want to say no. We may have said yes to avoid conflict, be nice, not disappoint, or meet expectations. Saying yes when we intend to say no is unhealthy and sourced from fear of rejection, a limiting belief. Thinking no but saying yes means their opinion of you matters more than your view of yourself. Saying no does not mean you don't care or are a terrible person; it means that you value your opinion of the best choice for you more than their view of you. Be intentional about saying yes by being aware of how the request aligns with your values and confirm that yes is the best choice for you. If not, confidently and politely say no.

4. Encircle yourself with family and friends who are positive, caring, and encouraging.

Your community has a lot to do with how you feel and think. Everyone does not deserve to have access to you or your time. Negativity in all forms promotes limiting beliefs and restricts your potential. Audit your close friends and influences by writing them down and taking inventory of the value each one brings to your life. Some people should be around you for a season, while others deserve to be in your life for a lifetime. Auditing your communities improves the mixture of people that can positively impact your perceived reality. Are there people that you are "fake" around or drain your energy? Let them go! As you become more connected with yourself, your intuition grows, and you become more aware of the things and people that do not align with your values.

Reaffirm your communities by reconnecting with healthy and positive relationships that make you smile. Are you projecting values that you would like to see in your community? Treat everyone—family, friend, or foe—with love, care, and respect, and your community will grow with people who want to share the same levels of love, care, and respect with you.

5. Refrain from comparing yourself to others.

Imagery taps into our emotions and affects our beliefs and thoughts. With the imposing presence that social media, television, music, beauty, and fitness have on our lives, it's difficult not to make upward comparisons. Comparing ourselves to people we believe are better than us induces lower self-love levels and a higher need for feedback. As William Shakespeare once wrote, "All that glisters is not gold." What we see as desirable through media outlets are snippets from a mastered highlight reel or digitalized snapshots of lives we'll never be able to emulate.

Many people we see as media idols and icons portray themselves as living sensational lives that do not exist as they hide their internal struggles and search for fulfillment. Social comparisons come from a place of lack and are attachments that detract from our authentic selves. Practice self-love and filter imagery from your perceived reality that promotes a scarcity mindset and self-doubt. Negative motivation from comparisons deliver unrealistic expectations and unnecessary disappointment.

Practicing self-love is at the base of discovering the best version of yourself. Celebrate all successes and victories, no matter how big or small! The more secure you are with yourself, the less you will be inclined to compare yourself to others. What is for others may not be for you, so be genuinely happy for them instead of envious. Be the remarkable adult like your parents intended by being happy and uniquely you.

TIME FOR REFLECTION

On a scale of 1 to 10 (10 being the highest), my level of happiness is a:

For every negative thought, I intend to review these three positive thoughts:

My self-love affirmations are:

I intend to audit my personal community by the following date:

My most recent victories and successes are:

PART II
Change Your Actions

CHAPTER SEVEN

Mask on Before Helping Others

"Your body is an amazing self-regulating, self-correcting wonder! Access its wisdom."
—Amy Leigh Mercree

WORKING WITH INVESTMENTS can be stressful, when there's little reason or minimal information on why the market moves up or down on a given day. Higher market volatility places investment professionals under pressure to quickly grasp what may be going on and advise clients on expectations.

During my early days of managing money, I was highly motivated to help clients achieve their financial goals. My workdays consisted of digesting news, assessing markets, trading investments, and checking in with clients. I wanted to shine like the brightest star on a cloudless night. For me, shining like a star meant rising before the sun, arriving to work early, leaving the office late, and flawlessly servicing as many client investment portfolios as I could each day.

Long days at the office turned into long nights. Lunches typically consisted of something quick and greasy from the local eateries. Fitness workouts were one of those great ideas that rarely became a reality. I thought about work on the way home, talked about work with anyone willing to listen, and dreamed about work every night.

I thoroughly enjoyed the world of investments, and a work-life balance did not matter much since I was grateful and happy with my role. Well, my friends, anything without moderation comes with a hefty price tag.

Before long, I felt ill. I consulted my doctor and then a specialist after days of discomfort and Mom's advice. The specialist exam-ined me and said many things, but I only heard three statements: "You have an autoimmune disease. Nobody knows what causes the condition. There is no cure." I pondered and reflected on the diagnosis. I spent weeks researching causes and remedies and even questioned the validity of the diagnosis. Some research suggested the condition originated with the consumption of certain foods and is stress-related. My findings were enough to motivate a holistic change to my lifestyle. Anything that may have been a solution to my ailment was fair game.

Favorable outcomes begin with a positive mindset, so I thanked God daily for the life I had and set the intention to heal. I repeated affirmations such as, "I am healthy. I am strong. I am resilient." whether I was in line at a grocery store or on my daily commute. I altered my eating habits to only include natural, whole, and unprocessed foods. I created time to run outdoors and held myself accountable to my fitness goals. I prioritized daily workloads, adhered to eight-hour days, took complete 60-minute lunch breaks, and created a manageable shortlist of daily tasks. My work did not follow me home, to bed, or enter outside of work conversations. I made an unbreakable barrier between work hours and "my time."

In less than a year after the diagnosis, I felt improvements. After clearing with the specialist, I discontinued medical treatment. It has been over fourteen years since the last dose of medication, and I have experienced no symptoms. I am grateful!

The body is magnificent and has an unmeasurable amount of resiliency that we subconsciously test over and over. We weaken our bodies with unhealthy diets, lack of exercise, and insufficient sleep. Mental, emotional, and physical stress negatively impact the optimal state of our internal functions. We allow ourselves to be attached to stressful work, draining relationships, and negative situations that disturb and disrupt our bodies' balance and harmony. We all know an overeager business or career-driven person who is, literally and figuratively, driving themselves to the grave. Is this you? If it is you, is it worth it?

Many of us pollute our bodies and decay our organs' vitality by consuming junk food, harmful drugs, and excessive alcohol. Could it be that of all the world forces that could kill us, we are the deadliest? Studies show that we can reduce our all-cause mortality risk by 66 percent by having a healthy lifestyle.[3] Consider the last time you were diagnosed with an illness or condition. The doctor inquired about your daily habits such as diet, exercise, and sleep, right? Lifestyle is the primary determinant of the quality of health and performance level for prevention and healing that we can achieve from our bodies. Healthy daily practices and habits can optimize our internal functions and prepare our bodies to prevent or heal when necessary. Just like a car needs gas, oil, and tires to drive effectively, your body needs nutritional foods, physical activity, and adequate sleep to raise your vibrational energy and positively influence your mental space and bodily functions. If we don't take care of ourselves, then, like a car, we will either break down or limit the ability to stay on the road. Replacing a faulty vehicle is possible, but replacing our unhealthy bodies is not.

Lower vibrational energy limits our ability to defend against bacteria, viruses, and infections that can cause harm or even death. A simple cold or prolonged exposure to the elements can lead to an

3 Earl S. Ford, Guixiang Zhao, James Tsai, et al, "Low-Risk Lifestyle Behaviors and All-Cause Mortality: Findings From the National Health and Nutrition Examination Survey III Mortality Study," NSBI, October 2011, https://www.ncbi.nlm.nih.gov/pmc/articles/PMC3222361/.

illness or condition, depending on our pre-existing health. Negative thoughts can affect how we feel and welcome biochemical critters into our bodies. The accumulation of stress, whether mental, emotional, or physical, can weaken our ability to prevent and heal. Stress elevates inflammation, which can seep into weaker areas in our bodies and cause health problems. Inflammation increases and breaks down our bodies as we age. Minor health issues become significant without adequately managing the causes of inflammation.

When we are not well, are we thinking positively or negatively? Do we wade in a pool of neediness when we feel unhealthy? Should an illness or condition determine our perceived reality?

We have the power to create an internal environment that encourages prevention and healing if we choose. Two people can have the same illness or condition but recover and heal differently. Differences occur with genetics and lifestyle, but how we vibrate, feel, and think can contribute to the recovering and healing process. The John Hopkins University of Medicine has completed studies on how positive thinking can impact our health. A recent study showed that individuals with a family background of heart illnesses and a positive mindset were 33 percent less likely to have respiratory failure or other cardiovascular limitations within the next five to twenty-five years than those who had negative views about their health.[4]

Positive emotions spark positive beliefs, thoughts, and actions and encourage prevention and healing. If we don't believe or think recovery is possible, our mindset is like a counterweight as our body attempts to heal itself. Sometimes, when we are in the depths of pain and discomfort, we don't feel or think about how negative emotions affect and delay the pace of our recovery and healing. If our

4 John Hopkins Medicine, "The Power of Positive Thinking," accessed March 6, 2021, https://www.hopkinsmedicine.org/health/wellness-and-prevention/the-power-of-positive-thinking.

energy, feelings, and thoughts align with our inner body recovery and healing, then we subconsciously assist with the process. Having an intentional success mindset applies to self-healing, just like any other topic. Medicine can fill in the gaps of what the body cannot do on its own, but the more self-healing that takes place, the less dependency we can have on medication.

Mom has always said, "Prevention is better than a cure." Feeding, exercising, and resting our bodies are more pleasant than treating, recovering, and healing from an illness or condition. When we feel achy, uneasy, sleepy, pain-ridden, or miserable, our inner bodies are working overtime to self-heal. Our bodies want to be healthy and in balance. Our lives are less challenging when we are well and in harmony!

Self-care is the best way to prevent illnesses, infections and promote self-healing. Let's take a moment to define and clarify the difference between self-care and self-healing. Self-care is the practice of maintaining our mental, emotional, and physical health. Self-healing is the mindful recovery process initiated by the conscious and subconscious minds. With proper self-care, we can prevent the need for self-healing and promote the quality and speed of self-healing. Self-care and self-healing go hand-in-hand. The more frequently we practice self-care, the less self-healing is necessary, and the greater the magnitude of self-healing that occurs when self-healing is essential.

PRACTICING SELF-CARE

The COVID-19 pandemic has influenced many of us to set aside time for self-care. Whether we are essential workers, working from home, or retired, we have modified our lifestyles. Some of us have embraced opportunities to focus on aspects of ourselves we commonly may have taken for granted. Surveys conducted during the pandemic show 80 percent of US respondents were more likely to practice self-care in some form after the pandemic.[5] Activities such as spending time outdoors, exercising meaningfully, eating healthier, and connecting with people on an authentic level increased among many households across America. The benefits are immeasurable! Self-care enables us to improve our emotional, mental, and physical health. The better we feel, the lower our stress levels and the more resilient our bodies and minds become.

1. Achieve a *life*-work balance.

You may find yourself working long days to complete to-do lists or taking work home, but you are capable of achieving balance and maintaining a healthier lifestyle. Instead of creating space in your career for your life, create space in your life for your career. Change your perspective, and your perceived reality changes. Make living your life the norm and prioritize your career as an activity to achieve balance like working out. Start by creating a schedule, delegating responsibilities, and intentionally saying yes to activities that support and enhance your mental, emotional, and physical health. Success arrives when we are living in balance and contribute our highest value to the task or activity at hand. Without our emotional, mental, and physical wellness, our happiness and success become limited or stagnant at work and home. Energy falls, and intentional focus drifts away from our action plans and goals when prompted to address unhealthy imbalances in our bodies. It's challenging to be happy when we're stressed, anxious, or depressed. It's challenging to succeed when we lack emotional and mental focus or distracted by our health.

Engage with at least one activity every day that you enjoy and achieve an emotional and mental release. Immerse yourself in

5 Joe Gramigna, "80% of Americans Intend to Regularly Practice Self-Care after COVID-19 Pandemic," Healio, June 12, 2020, https://www.healio.com/news/psychiatry/20200612/80-of-americans-intend-to-regularly-practice-selfcare-after-covid19-pandemic.

activities you enjoy, such as spending time with loved ones, a massage, a wonderful book, Bible study, bubble bath, going for a walk, or mindful meditation. Select pleasurable activities that create space for you to quiet the mind, recenter unbalanced emotions, and achieve inner peace. Having a life-work balance minimizes the accumulation of stress, rests the mind and body, and collectively prepares us for optimal performance.

2. Eat nutritiously.

Eating has become a transactional activity to address hunger until the time arrives for the next meal. Some of us eat to pass the time, and others view eating as an activity for continued survival and health. The food choices you make determine how your body processes and transforms energy into fuel for the inner and physical body. If you eat low nutritional value foods, the mind and body will operate at inefficient levels, limiting vibrational energy that supports positive feelings, thoughts, and actions.

Don't put rocks in the gas tank, and expect the car to run like it's on premium fuel. A balanced diet rich in nutrients poises the inner and physical bodies to operate at a superior level when necessary.

Lean on resources to get you on the right track with your eating habits. Read books, listen to podcasts, or subscribe to health publications to increase your knowledge about nutritious foods and improve your eating habits. Technology can be helpful as well. Several nutrition apps can help you stay on the path to wellness, such as:

- MyFitnessPal — Helps with nutrition, losing weight, and eating habits.
- MyNetDiary — Helps track calories, exercise, and food.
- SuperFood — Provides superfood recipes.

3. Commit to enjoyable physical fitness activities.

Walking, running, cycling, yoga, aerobics, Pilates, dance, weight-lifting, and high-intensity interval training (HIIT) can make a difference in your wellness when included as an essential part of your lifestyle. Some of us need a structure, like a fitness class or coach, dently. Either way, we must hold ourselves accountable to achieve consistent results and be present during every workout session to be effective. Plan out your workout schedule ahead of time and view working out like going out to recess as you did as a child. Unleash your mind, just be, and have fun! Working out is as good for your mental space as it is for you physically.

When we mindfully engage in physical activity, we release stress accumulations that interfere with the immune system and increase inflammation levels. Moderate physical activity can strengthen the immune system by pushing out bacteria and toxins to stave off infections. Cardio activities increase blood flow and oxygen, which replenishes energy stores that prime the mind and body for restful sleep.

Most forms of physical activity are beneficial in some way to your overall health. You've probably never heard anyone say that they felt worst after exercising. Why is that? Physical activity allows the brain to produce "feel-good" chemicals known as endorphins that elevate mood. Some of us may call the euphoria a "runner's high," or that may be just me. Self-care in the form of physical activity is essential to preventing illness and strengthening our self-healing abilities. Be sure to consult with your physician to understand what physical activities may be best for you!

Examples of fitness apps:

- Glo — Has instructor-led yoga and meditation sessions for all levels.

- Johnson & Johnson Official 7 Minute Workout — Includes short circuit training workouts with varying intensities.
- Keelo — Contains on-demand HIIT workouts.

4. Establish an almost non-negotiable sleep schedule.

Sleep is not just for kids and senior citizens. Adequate sleep supports healthy weight, mood, memory, heart, and stress levels. Lack of sleep limits success by affecting concentration and productivity. Restful sleep can remove toxins from the brain and body and allow recovery from the day's activities. The number of hours of sleep to perform optimally differs by person and the day's activities. At a minimum, we should set a sleep schedule that allows us to receive six to eight hours of sleep. Studies have shown that consistently skipping sleep leads to a 25 percent decrease in brain cells.[6] Think about the greatness we can achieve with all of those lost brain cells!

Bad days can be better days, and good days can be great days with enough sleep. Rest is one of the easiest habits to neglect but can be the most impactful hidden contributor to our happiness and success. Apple and Android devices have a sleep-tracking feature that keeps you honest with your hours of sleep and allows you to set up a sleep schedule. Allocate time and effort to figure out the optimal number of hours of sleep required based on your activities and schedule. Plan your life around your sleep schedule and allow sleep to positively contribute to how you feel, think, and move.

Self-care is critical to our minds and bodies. Everyone is busy, but caring for ourselves is just as important as when we care for ourselves. Daily self-care rituals in the morning, midday, and evenings can influence the quality of our lives. After a stressful day, relaxing in the evening may significantly affect our bodies, lowering inflammation, more than waiting for the weekend.

6 Helen Briggs, "Lost Sleep Leads to Loss of Brain Cells, Study Suggests," BBC News, March 19, 2014, https://www.bbc.com/news/health-26630647.

Eating unhealthy food or binge-drinking alcohol eventually affects our minds and bodies, limiting our ability to thrive mentally, emotionally, and physically. Change your lifestyle gradually for sustainable results. Start by eating healthier, sleeping more, and finding a workout routine that works best for you. The better you take care of your body, the better your body takes care of you.

When self-care is a priority, your mental, emotional, and physical health starts from an beneficial state when an illness or infection looms. Change your mindset and actions, practice self-care, and your body's ability to self-heal improves.

TIME FOR REFLECTION

On a scale of 1 to 10 (1 being nonexistent), my life-work balance is:

I intend to achieve life-work balance by:

I intend to improve my physical fitness by:

I intend to do one activity per day that will help me with self-care:

To have a healthy body, I intend to decrease my intake of:

To have a strong body, I intend to do the following exercise:

To improve my sleep schedule, I intend to:

CHAPTER EIGHT

Wishful Thinking Is Just the Beginning

"Ask for what you want and be prepared to get it."
—Maya Angelou

TWELVE DAYS BEFORE my seventh Christmas, I knew in my heart there was going to be a red BMX bike beside the tree on Christmas morning! I had written a letter to Santa in August to give Santa and his elves time to locate the bike. I could see the bike as vividly in my mind today as I could back then! I requested a red bike with an aluminum frame, plastic pedals, and pro-handlebar grips, plus front and rear freestyle pegs. The joy that arrived with every thought of my Christmas gift constantly ran through my body. I could see myself on the bike and doing freestyle stunts with my friends.

Mom asked me what was on my Christmas list every year and encouraged me to be on my best behavior so Santa would acknowledge my requests. To do my part and make my visions a reality, I focused on being a good kid, helping my parents, and showing goodwill to Santa every day. I lived my life with no doubt the red BMX was mine. As children, we were the ultimate manifesters! We had no resources but knew how to be resourceful and creative with our energy and imagination.

Manifestation, for our purposes, is using spirituality to incite emotions, thoughts, and actions to make something theoretical *real.* What happens to our manifesting ability as we become adults? The power of manifestation remains within us, but our beliefs, experiences, and observations have narrowed the breadth of our imaginations. We have created mental walls and limited successful manifestation outcomes to the extent that goal-setting and action-planning allow. We have attached ourselves to high probable results and only attempt safe bets, which has muted our freeing ability to manifest anything we desire.

For some of us, goal-setting and action-planning alone have not been enough to materialize outcomes as expected. We laid out goals and calculated steps but need more to believe and see to overcome distractions and disruptions. To give us the extra nudge, spiritually connecting with something greater than yourself—such as God, the universe, cocreator, Santa Claus, or whatever you soulfully believe—can empower us to achieve more than ever imagined. The manifestation goal-achieving concept is simple, but in practice can be difficult if our energy, emotions, mindset, and actions are not in alignment with the request. How do we make manifestation simple? We have to be mentally and spiritually prepared to receive what we ask.

The defining principle of manifestation is that we are the cocreators of our perceived reality through self-awareness and spirituality. We can intentionally bring people, places, things, and experiences physically into our lives based on the energy, thoughts, and actions we direct toward a desire, goal, or outcome. Prayers and manifestations require a high level of faith that the expected result will materialize as requested. Prosperous blessings and manifestations cannot occur without complete confidence in the process and surrender of the desired outcome. Beliefs and thoughts filled with doubt, neediness, manipulation, or control limit us in every way.

Faith cannot exist in the presence of doubt. Manifestations appear when we are consciously ready to receive, and our actions center on people, experiences, and things that align with our desires.

I was not familiar with the concept of manifestation when I requested the red BMX, but my energy, thoughts, and actions were in alignment with the request which delivered the bike. Sending the request to Santa and having visual imagery, limitless beliefs, and thoughts that determined aligned actions invited the bike into my life. Our desires must be real *within* us before they can be *for* us. I had complete trust in Santa and was confident that my thoughts and actions were in alignment with the request. Santa, better known as Mom, took care of the rest.

Manifestation is not wishful thinking. We are preparing our minds to create space for a clear vision to recognize opportunities that can bring what we desire to us. We cannot ask for a house and expect it to appear. With manifesting a house, the process may include:

- visualizing every detail of the home you desire;
- reviewing homes that align with your expectations;
- making a specific spiritual request;
- saving for a down payment; and
- improving debt balances.

Manifestation requests are successful when we're specific and subconsciously believe, without a doubt, that our manifestation is going to arrive. If we are consciously dwelling on what we want, subconsciously fearing disappointment, and physically taking self-sabotaging actions, we block the pathway to a successful outcome. A scarcity mindset blocks abundance, and a success mindset deliver abundance.

Many of us lose faith in manifestation practices because we believe that unwavering hope or asking our spiritual connection for what we want is all it takes. We will become disappointed and frustrated with that approach since no magic wand or pixie dust can deliver our request. Making the request, spiritually, is the beginning. Intentional focus on the necessary steps to take advantage of the opportunities that align with our manifestations invite success.

MANIFESTING WHAT YOU WANT

Several steps lead to successful manifestation, and each step is essential to achieve the desired outcome. You have everything you need within you to have whatever you want in life. If you can believe it, feel it, think it, and see it, you can have it! Does that sound unbelievably easy? Let's find out.

1. Be crystal clear about your desire.

Anything we desire to be real begins with a thought. Let's consider manifesting a job. If you want to manifest a new job, then be specific with your thoughts about the position you seek. What kind of job aligns with your values and brings fulfillment? Where is the job located? If you want the job to be in your current city, then say so. How will the job bring you intentional success? Write out the details. "A job that pays good money" should not be in the details. Explicitly write how *much* money. What do you want to do to earn the desired amount of money? Again, be specific. Reference what you want, not what you don't want. Describe the job as if you already have it. What are your duties?

The aim here is to ensure that your thoughts are not coming from a place of want or need but abundance. As you write about your dream job, describe the job in simple terms to someone who may not understand it. As you solidify your request with thought reinforced by limitless beliefs, positive emotions begin to center on the manifestation. Beliefs steer feelings; feelings encourage thought, thoughts prompt actions, and actions lead to results. What we think about, we invite into our life.

Place the request with your spiritual connection with an open mind and positive thoughts once you are clear on what you want.

2. Surrender control.

This step in the manifestation process marks that we have made our request and are ready to let go of the outcome. We are not letting go of what we want; we are letting go of doubt, timing, and outcome. Surrendering control is the most challenging step in the manifestation process. We as human beings spend thought and energy attempting to control the future. Why waste our thoughts and energy on what we cannot control? We can only control outcomes in the present. When we focus our thoughts and actions on the present, we uncover greater opportunities and execute advancing tasks that deliver our goals. We limit happiness and success by forfeiting the present for the past or future.

Have you had an experience that turned out to be better than expected? Letting go of how an experience is should turn out allows mindset and actions to permit the experience to unfold as intended. Eleven-time NBA Championship coach and author Phil Jackson said, "The most we can hope for is to create the best possible conditions for success, then let go of the outcome. The ride is a lot more fun that way." Surrender control, trust the process, and be present in every moment to experience a positive manifestation result—an approach that provides a reward far more significant than our imagination than if we dwell on the outcome.

Have you ever studied(read and memorize) versus learned (knowledge and skill) the material to pass an exam? The intention to pass the exam is the same whether we study or learn, but there is a difference in the perceived control and general mindset. Let me explain. We study the material for an exam because we believe we have control over passing the exam, the future. We learn the material for an exam because we believe we can master exam concepts, the present. See the difference? Strength grows where focus goes. Studying places emphasis on passing the exam. Learning places emphasis on knowledge to pass the exam. The two exam preparation approaches illustrate the differences between scarcity and success mindsets. Which approach aligns better with the intention of passing an exam? Today, we must focus on the highest value activity that can unleash the expected outcome we deserve tomorrow. Manifestations work when we surrender control and take actions toward our manifestation in the present.

3. Use affirmations and visualize for subconscious clarity.

For manifestations, we can use powerful affirmations to trigger positive emotion and help the subconscious mind remain on track for our manifestations. Keep the affirmations short, so they're easy to remember and recite.

Examples of powerful affirmations are below, but you can also review the affirmations in chapter one:

- I trust in the process.
- I release all fear and doubt toward my manifestations.
- I am intentionally successful in all that I do.
- I am confident and motivated for success.
- I am creating the life I want.

Review affirmations to erode limiting beliefs filled with fear and doubt. The higher vibrational energy that accompanies reciting affirmations increases confidence and replaces negative thoughts. Positive energy, emotions, and thoughts evoked by affirmations smother feelings of lack and allow you to carry on with your life as if you already have everything you want and need.

To take this concept a step further, imagine or visualize that the request has already happened with the same confidence as knowing you have a birthday every year. See the house you manifested with the specific details you requested. Believe that the house is yours to the same degree your birthday is on the date you were born.

4. Action, action, action.

Successful manifestation outcomes are possible with action. Manifestation is a cocreating process that requires us to hold up our end of the deal with aligned actions. Actions close the gap between where you are and want to be and convey to your spiritual connection that you are serious about your intention. Plan and execute the next action step that will enable you to progress toward your goal. Don't procrastinate or try to be perfect. Both limit progress. If you're unsure of your next step, connect with subject matter experts—people who are familiar with the outcome you are seeking. Use resources such as books and online videos to provide clarity. Take intentional action and pursue opportunities that excite you. Entirely focus on each step toward your goal. Be present in your life and mindfully open to engaging with opportunities.

5. Be happy.

You have made the request, affirmed your desire, let go of the outcome, visualized the manifestation, and took actions toward your manifested goal. Enjoy the journey!

We have to carry on with our daily lives by living in the moment and not thinking about whether our manifested goal is on its way. Stop checking the metaphorical mailbox for the delivery! If you know in your heart that you are being mindful and executing the steps to get you there, there is no need to cloud your mind by dwelling on the request. Dwelling creates negative thoughts. Be happy and trust the process! Revisit your affirmations, visualize, and express gratitude daily to reposition your mind in a positive state as thoughts of lack emerge. The higher our vibrational energy and happier we are, the more likely we are to invite positive experiences and take actions that lead our manifestation to us.

If you're new to intentional manifesting, start small and manifest one desire at a time. Manifest small things such as helping your teen improving their high school GPA by .25 by the end of the semester or having an extra $100 that you add to your savings by month-end. Be specific. As your confidence increases, move on to more prominent manifestations. By starting small, your subconscious mind replaces doubt with greater certainty. As the more minor manifestations become a reality, vibrational energy transforms into emotions that strengthen our beliefs and expectations.

Think of your subconscious mind as a strengthening muscle that becomes stronger through reps, similar to lifting weights in a gym. We start with lighter weights and move up to heavier weights. As we become physically stronger, our faith increases in the amount of weight we can manage. The same is true with manifestation. We emotionally and mentally fortify our beliefs and trust in the process as they become reinforced with favorable outcomes. Manifest small and move up as it becomes easier to achieve alignment and favorable results.

As you move on to more extensive or life-changing manifestations, a practice that may help replace limiting beliefs and subconscious doubts is scripting. Scripting is the act of writing a creative story from the imagination, as if you've already received the manifestation. Scripting elevates energy and generates emotions filled with positivity to create the story. Going beyond affirmation statements and targeting the feelings associated with achieving the manifestation is the secret ingredient to successful scripting and manifestation.

Scripting works when positive energy and emotions are present as you write. There must not be any doubt or contradictory thoughts present for scripting to be practical. Otherwise, the scripted words look good on paper but do not meet the purpose of scripting. This concept reminds me of people who go to church and expect blessings solely by the act of going to church. Action alone provides limited results. It is the energy, emotions, beliefs, and thoughts that align with the actions that lead to expected outcomes. Scripting is a successful exercise when there are positive energy and feelings behind the words on the page.

So how do you script? To start, purchase a journal where the pages are in a bounded spine. I suggest a bounded-type collection of paper rather than a spiral or perforated notebook since the latter gives us a sense of temporary. The spiraled or perforated spine means pages can be removed or are temporarily in the notebook. Evolving and changing our limiting beliefs should not be temporary, or at least that should not be the intention. Positive and affirmed beliefs should be everlasting and become core to who we are. If we're going to change our hardwired subconscious limiting beliefs permanently, our environment should support and reinforce the transformation.

This idea is the same when selecting a writing instrument for your journal. Use a permanent ink pen and not a pencil or an erasable ink pen. We have the will to commit to our growth by observing and understanding and letting go of our flaws. If you need to correct something that you script, cross it out and keep it moving.

Some of us choose journals that are fancy or have intricate designs on the cover that have meaning in some form, while others buy the cheapest, most basic journal. Do what aligns with who you are. Dedicate a chosen journal and pen for scripting. You should feel good about your choice of journal and pen. If writing in purple ink floats your boat, write in purple ink. If a journal that says something meaningful on the cover makes you feel fantastic, purchase a journal with a meaningful saying on the surface. Your manifestation's success is not on the journal's exterior or the amount of money you spend on the journal.

Success depends on how you feel about the experience and the actions you take. Your manifestation results will be favorable if scripting begins and ends with powerful beliefs and positive emotion. Scripting creates space for awareness and reflection.

Scripting journal entries can be a letter or story. It's totally up to you. There is no wrong way to do scripting journal entries as long the entries are written in the present tense and come from positivity. Refrain from thoughts of doubt and negative self-talk. Journaling should be fun and just for you, so don't get hung up on the format, sentence structure, or paragraph length. I suggest that your journal entries start with a date and statements of gratitude and end with an "I am" affirmation statement or two. Beginning with the date memorializes the journal entry, allowing you to revisit the entry and reflect. Gratitude encourages positive thoughts and helps you get in a flow or zone—mentally immersed with abundance. Affirmations are there to declare what you feel to be accurate as you bring your entry to a close.

Realize that your manifestations may or may not arrive when you expect or in the order as you requested. That's okay. Be grateful anyway—acknowledgment and gratitude for when and what does come is part of the journey. Expressions of appreciation elevate vibrational energy and should appear throughout your journal entries. The power of scripting resides in emotion. Below are three sample scripted letter entries to help you brainstorm:

> *Thank you so much for the fantastic new house. The bedrooms are the perfect size for my two boys, and the master closet is just the right size for my many dresses*

and husband's business suits. My husband just loves cooking up the perfect gourmet meals in our beautiful kitchen, where everything is within reach or stored within the vast center island with the gorgeous quartz countertop.

Today, my girlfriend and I are at a new restaurant that we heard is so amazing. As we walk in, the hostess greets us as if we are the most beautiful couple she has ever seen. As we walk to our table, my girlfriend reaches for my hand as if she felt I was too far away. I look at her with pure adoration as we arrive at the table and pull her chair to be seated while making sure she has somewhere to place her handbag securely. Thank you for blessing me with a loving relationship and a girlfriend that unconditionally cares for me as much as I care for her.

I am so happy that I am finally doing what I love, running a successful event planning business. The bookings fill up the calendar as every day passes by, and the reviews have been better than I could ever imagine! Patrons are booking services six to eight months in advance to experience a one-of-a-kind event that will be memorable for all guests in attendance. Thank you for the vision, motivation, and patience to be intentional with my thoughts and actions and build a phenomenal business from the ground up.

Scripting journal entries are like hypnotic writing where you are mentally and emotionally so involved with every word as you write. The ink flows as you feel excited with each lift of the pen to write another word or sentence.

If your thoughts slow or lack feeling, write a statement of gratitude or affirmation to refocus emotion and clear the mind. Scripting is like growing a plant. Roots from a planted seed cannot succeed unless they receive water and nourishment to flourish. Review your scripted journal entries daily to develop positive emotions and thoughts and replace limiting beliefs.

If you prefer, write mini-journal entries daily about the manifestation instead of reviewing the same journal entry repeatedly. What are the best times to review journal entries for you? A recommended time to review and write journal entries is before bed or as you wake up in the morning when the subconscious mind is more active.

The only thing that can prevent you from achieving all that you desire is your mindset! Scripting is one of the most powerful practices you can do to achieve alignment with your goal and increase confidence that your manifestation is on its way!

TIME FOR REFLECTION

I intend to strengthen the relationship with my spiritual connection by:

I intend to manifest the following goal in my life:

I intend to surrender control and enjoy the journey rather than the outcome by:

I intend to take action as I manifest my goal by:

I intend to practice scripting the following:

CHAPTER NINE

Seeing Leads to Believing

"You can't do anything that you can't picture yourself doing. Once you make the picturing process conscious and deliberate, you begin to create the self you want to be."

—Anonymous

MANY OF US have leadership aspirations as we matriculate through our careers and desire to increase the value we add to organizations. As we become experienced and specialized in our respective fields, we target leadership positions and hope that people retire or move elsewhere so we can occupy their coveted roles.

I wanted to be in leadership at my firm, but the leadership position I desired was not available, and I didn't have the experience required for the role. As a go-getter, this revelation did not present obstacles but a challenge to prepare for the next level. I saw myself as the CEO and desired the opportunity to show an organization that I am the CEO. Since I had no actual plan other than leaving the organization to obtain leadership experience, my mentor suggested I look outside of my firm's organizational chart. Not knowing what that entailed, I reached out to volunteer organizations aligned with my values and goals. Connecting with nonprofit and community organizations that aligned with my interests was exciting and opened my eyes to unlimited possibilities.

I applied to join the board of directors of a local Charlotte nonprofit organization that served at-risk youth by providing tutoring, mentoring, sports, camps, intervention, and community services. The opportunity to inspire and guide children, emotionally and economically challenged, to become positive members of society appealed to me. Most of these children do not have positive role models in their communities or receive the support to improve their trajectory in life. Where would my life be without positive role models or support to be my best?

To apply for a nonprofit organization's board of directors without prior leadership experience was daunting. I spoke with people serving on other boards and researched the organization inside and out to boost my confidence before applying. During the interview, I received questions on topics such as effective board governance, risk management, and ethical practices. The funny thing is I provided textbook responses off the top of my head. I had been learning about sound corporate governance for an investment designation exam! The universe works in amazing ways. The board president contacted me days later to attend the upcoming board meeting to be confirmed.

I attended the board meeting and saw other board candidates attending as well. The board president introduced the other candidates and moved to vote them on the board. A board member seconded, and the remaining board members voted in favor. My heart began to sink. The board president didn't introduce me, nor was a motion made to vote me on the board. Suddenly I didn't understand why I was there. In the middle of my internal pity party, the board president said she would like to introduce Mr. Namaine Coombs to the board. By this time, I was doing a happy dance in my head as she shared highlights from the interview with the board. Just when I thought a board vote was about to begin, the board president voiced that she would like to step down as board president and nominate Mr. Coombs to replace her as board president.

Wait. What?

I didn't have formal leadership experience, never have been on a board of directors, and now I am being asked to *lead* a board of directors? Wow!

When we're clear on our vision, it becomes simple to decide. I accepted the nomination without hesitation, was voted on the board, and received the agenda to run the meeting.

Item three on the agenda was a proposal for a charter school. The former board president presented a proposal to expand the nonprofit organization into a charter school for grades five through eight. I had no children, knew nothing about charter schools, and now expected to lead a nonprofit organization to build a charter school. Sign me up! I saw myself as a CEO, and now I can demonstrate my ability to lead an organization.

I led the nonprofit's board of directors to complete the state's required charter school application, obtain funding sources, and achieve a unanimous charter approval vote from the state's board of education. The doors of the charter school opened later that year. Today, the school has been open for five years serving grades five through twelve, and I am still the governing board president. I achieved the goal of being in leadership by *seeing* myself and behaving like a CEO of an organization well before *leading* an organization. If you can see it and believe it, anything you want is possible!

Visualization or mental imagery can positively shape the subconscious mind. Images stimulate emotion and thought that could trigger action. The feelings present when seeing a joyful newborn differ from when visiting a violent car wreck. Both visuals prompt different emotions and thoughts that initiate different actions. We must choose our visuals wisely.

Visualization is the critical component in achieving anything in life. There is nothing human-made in this world that exists without first being imagined. As you recall, the subconscious mind cannot separate what is real from what we imagine.

Maurice Koechlin and Émile Nouguier, the engineers and designers of the Eiffel Tower in France, visualized the structure well before the drafting pencils hit the paper. Athletes visualize seeing and feeling at peak performance as if the game or competition has already occurred. Musicians imagine their entire performance note by note to calm jitters and nervousness as they mentally prepare to wow fans. Surgeons visualize operating on their patient, from placing the incision to the intricate details of the targeted internal anatomy to suturing the opening with precision, well before heading into the operating room.

Creating visual imagery in the conscious mind transforms energy into emotions that can drive success with each step toward our goal. If your goal is to be the top salesperson at your firm, imagine the steps to build your brand and increase your win rate. Whatever imagery you intended to project in your mind, be specific about the details and leave nothing to chance. My motivation and success would have been different if my visualizations of being a leader were general or lacked detail.

I was passionate about children and leading an organization that aligned with my values, which replaced limiting beliefs and expanded the possibilities. The higher our vibrational energy and the greater the emotions directed toward the goal, the more intentional our mindset and actions can become. We have to be deliberate on the details of our visualization to have a positive emotional impact on our thoughts and actions. How do energy and emotion drive action? By operating at higher vibrational frequencies, we can spark the level of emotion necessary to give us confidence in the outcome we desire. We have to trust the process and see past the doubt and obstacles. Higher confidence increases with focus. Heightened focus introduces planning and actionable opportunities that enable us to achieve goals with plans and actions that align with our values. We experience resistance when our life, feelings, attitude, and activities misalign with our plans. Resistance blocks abundance by promoting negative emotions and thoughts through limiting beliefs.

Visualization is successful with constant reinforcement. Every night and morning, I thought about the school's details and visualized the school bell ringing, children in classrooms learning, and children smiling on graduation day. Developing reinforcing positive emotions and a success mindset can be difficult because of our brains' negative biases. If we cannot visualize ourselves being successful, low vibes, negative emotions, and a scarcity mindset confine our actions. See yourself achieving your goals as intended. Positive imagery gives strength and purpose to our destinations by removing doubt from our belief system and instilling confidence that our goals are on the way.

Visualization and the art of manifestation are not replacements for work and perseverance. They are conscious prompts to align emotion, thought, and action with our goals. Visualization is a superpower we never acknowledged we had. As with any superpower, use visualization with care. If we visualize unfavorable situations or outcomes, we invite negativity and lower consciousness levels into our perceived reality.

Living and feeling that the goal's achievement is happening give our goals legs to come to us. If I could not see myself as a leader of an organization, the mission to transform a nonprofit into a charter school would have been impossible. With any manifestation, favorable outcomes are plausible when our goals and desires pair with a success mindset. We have to see ourselves as capable, creative, and resourceful to unleash intentional success. Feelings of want or lack cloud the mind and block the flow of unlimited possibilities. A mind clouded with lack does not have space to receive information that may provide the path for intentional success. Intentionally imagining ourselves being at our best and achieving our desires instills clarity and confidence. We can see and take advantage of the steps, actions, and resources that align with the goal.

Setting intentions and affirming our beliefs with powerful words invite what is for us and lays the groundwork for a successful plan with intentional action. Without higher vibrational energy, positive emotion, and confirming thoughts, we can self-sabotage what is for us with nonproductive efforts. Visualization and aligned actions deliver continuity between what we want, feel, and think and our successful outcomes.

VISUALIZING YOUR NEW REALITY

You have the power to be and do anything when you can see yourself carrying out aligned actions and achieving your desires. Visualization requires critical steps to transform you from being a dreamer to a believer, from a believer to a doer. What you can see, you can receive.

1. Be clear on what you want and why.

For effective visualization to occur, energy, emotion, and thought must focus on a single idea. We authentically connect and invite what we want into our lives by understanding why we want what we want. Intentions matter. As you consider a goal, reflect on why you want the outcome. What is driving your focus toward that goal?

When I visualized myself as a leader of an organization, it wasn't because it was a neat thing to do. I intended to lead with purpose and create immense value for the organization. Developing goals with intention subconsciously embeds the thought and convinces our minds that the goal will happen. Have you ever wanted something, and after receipt, the outcome was less than imagined? The outcome differs from thought because the "why" was not clear. Research as much as possible about what you desire to uncover your why.

If you want a promotion, why do you want a promotion?

What would you accomplish with the additional responsibilities?

Many of us are impatient about promotions, but it is not the title that defines us. It is the value we deliver. Skills and credentials are not enough. Deliver the highest value in your current role, and promotion opportunities arrive as recognition instead of a feat. There's a difference. As Simon Sinek, author of *Start with Why*, explains, "People don't buy what you do; they buy why you do it." The more value you deliver to increase the firm's value, the harder you make it for management and other firms to overlook your efforts. Focus on why you want the expected outcome. Visualize what you can do today to deliver the most incredible value to prepare for the desired result. Be clear with your images, and better decisions and outcomes will follow.

2. Be detailed about your goal.

The purpose of imagery is to activate the subconscious mind and expand our perceived realities. Visualization inspires our beliefs and thoughts to get them on board with our desires and solidify the possibilities. Success has to begin in the mind before it can be an outcome.

Write your goal or manifestation and describe. If your goal is to be a Realtor, be specific about the type of Realtor? Are you selling commercial or residential properties? Who are your customers or clients? Where would your office be located? Perhaps you have a street or physical address in mind. The more specific we are, the more detailed our visuals will be, and the less that is left for chance. Writing and thinking about what you want sparks emotion, priming the mind for optimal imagery.

3. Be at one with your mind.

We spend time in our heads, talking ourselves into and out of things daily. Internal dialogue can make it challenging to direct energy and gain focus. Personally, a long outdoor run creates mental space for direction and support mental imagery. Some of my most excellent emotional but motivating moments occurred on a long-distance run. For some of us, sitting in a silent room with eyes closed quiets the mind. Others may want to do a random brain dump by writing down everything on our mind to create space for focused thought. When we have no more to write, we are ready to focus on our goal and visualize. Visualization requires mental clarity and deliberate concentration to clear conscious noise. A mindful meditation session can help prepare us to visualize. Mental space enables the opportunity for focus, feeling, and visuals.

4. Begin to see and believe.

Think of the art of visualization as mentally rehearsing for the actual outcome like a football team watching a film leading up to a big game. Visualization is a mental run-through of the expected result.

Intentionally select quiet times of the day, such as minutes before going to bed or just as you wake in the morning, to practice visualization. Moments before falling asleep and after rising are when the conscious mind is the least active and the subconscious mind is the most active. Discover the time of day that works best for you. Visualization should occur daily and consistently, same visuals over and over, to be compelling.

Review the details of your goal. Close your eyes and imagine everything there is to conceive about the goal. If you visualize a motorcycle, see the reflections on the chrome and hear the throttling engine growl. If the goal centers on you, see yourself achieving the goal from a third-person point of view. Create a movie in your mind with surround sound and fantastic cinematography. Your visuals match the energy you have for your goal: the more energy, the more vivid the imagery, the more emotions generated to inspire intentional actions.

5. Bring the action.

Visualization is not rocket science, but it's useless without action. Visualizing daily, even just for a few minutes, can raise energy and increase positive emotions to start feelings, thought, and activities that align with successful outcomes. We as humans use visualization intentionally and haphazardly. We draw triumphs and tribulations into our lives without being conscious of our accountability for the outcomes. Use visualization to fire you up and motivate you to do whatever it takes to bring your manifested goal into your life. Productive visualization creates momentum to emotionally and mentally position us to unleash intentional success. Many chapters of this book materialized as I wrote each word while sitting in a bookstore. I took breaks to visit the self-help section and visualize this book on the shelf. Aligned imagery strengthens the success mindset, but nothing happens without aligned actions. Visualization is as good as daydreaming if there is no action. Creativity and motivation expand as we live out the images we visualize.

Whether you're setting an intention or reciting an affirmation, visualize your outcomes as intended and affirmed. If you set the intention to spend time with family, imagine yourself spending time with family. Think about how great you feel when you're with family. See yourself enjoying activities you love doing together as if time no longer exists. If you affirm that you're in a loving relationship, imagine the butterflies-in-your-stomach type of feeling when you're loved and giving love. By seeing with consistency, we minimize room for doubt.

To supplement daily visualization practices, a vision board can help.

A vision board is a visual aid to bring focus to any goal or desire. They consist of a collection of pictures, cutouts, and affirmations that emotionally resonate and reinforce your will to commit. For example, a picture of the car you want drives emotion when added to a vision board. Mom had a German sedan on her "vision board," also known as the refrigerator, and now she owns the sedan. Let's say you have a goal of traveling to Europe, place pictures of the hotel where you want to stay, locations you want to visit, and a picture of your packed suitcase. The more connections you have with the board, the better! Many of us use bulletin or whiteboards as our vision boards, but use whatever is pleasing to you. Select a board that you'll look forward to reviewing.

The concept of a vision board is to bring focus and connect realism to your ideas. Vision boards prompt you to imagine the outcome as if it's happening now. You have what you want! It's on your board. The images connecting with your subconscious mind increase confidence and erodes doubt. The vision board helps maintain motivation and perspective.

If we research vision boards, we'll see various examples and types that serve different purposes. Not all vision boards are subliminally impactful for success. Visualization is impactful when we achieve clarity and can focus our emotions and thoughts on an image. This concept of visualization applies to vision boards as well. Your board should be uncluttered, clear-cut, and goal-centric. A board that has unrelated ideas or multiple goals, or lacks intentional focus limits its effectiveness. A vision board assembled in a disorderly manner invites chaos and detracts from directing emotion and thought toward a single goal or desire. Clutter creates energy leaks. Our energy is impactful when mindfully concentrated.

Energy and emotion mold the beliefs of the subconscious mind into thoughts and actions that lead to success. When we simultaneously place energy, emotion, and thought into multiple goals, the probability of achieving a goal as intended is compromised. You can have various goals but assemble the vision board to focus on one goal at a time. It's more challenging to focus on multiple objects than to focus on a single object.

CREATING A VISION BOARD

Creating a vision board is an experience that triggers positive thoughts and emotions that amplify as you connect with the vision board. To get you started on your vision board, I will share a description of mine. My vision board had affirmations for the charter school, such as, "I am leading with purpose. I am providing the kids with the education they deserve. I am grateful to influence the mission of an organization that aligns with my values." Pictures include smiling children with backpacks and books, classrooms and school buses, the skyline of downtown Charlotte, the school building to purchase, and the board members' headshots. The school's mission statement and motivational quotes are on the board's outer perimeter.

1. Select or construct a visually appealing board.

Purchase or build a board that has a surface and frame that appeals to you. Your vision board is an imagery portal into the subconscious mind.

2. Gather materials to design your board.

Without a vision, there is no success. Design your vision board with related pictures, words, phrases, affirmations, and quotes. If you do not feel joy, love, or peace with your board's selected items, find other visuals.

3. Assemble your vision board.

Visualize how you would like to review your vision board daily. Start by placing your affirmations. Read each affirmation out loud as inspiration as you fasten the affirmations to the board. Look at the pictures or images you have gathered. Do they excite you about your goal? More images do not mean better. Think quality over quantity. What about quotes, words, and phrases? Layer them in where they enlighten you. Accomplish the goal of assembling the board with intention, and everything after that will purposely fall in place.

4. Select an accessible location for your vision board.

Where you place the vision board determines its effectiveness. Locate the vision board in a prominent area like an office or bedroom. The visual aspect of seeing your vision board subconsciously and often inspires you to take action. Do not dwell on the vision board with thoughts of neediness or lack. A scarcity mindset pushes our goals farther away.

As you achieve each goal, celebrate your accomplishments and reflect on the board to remind yourself about the milestones and the journey. As you reflect, confidence grows, and you become empowered to take on the next goal. You can remove the images and move to the next goal or use a different board for each goal. If you prefer to use the same vision board over and over, clear the board and assemble affirmations and images for your new goal. It is your vision and vision board, so own it!

TIME FOR REFLECTION

The goal I want to visualize is:

I intend to prepare my mind to visualize my goal by:

When I picture my goal, I see:

I intend to have my vision board and add images of the following by:

I intend to put my vision board where I can see it by:

CHAPTER TEN

A Quiet Mind Is the Best Mind

"Quiet the mind, and the soul will speak."
—Ma Jaya Sati Bhagavati

THE SUN IS up, so I am up! As I awake from a restful night of sleep, my eyes spring open with excitement to experience another perfect day. I look over at the clock and see 5:33, which means there is more than enough time before my feet need to hit the floor. I then sit upright, slide down to the southernmost edge of the bed, place my feet on the floor, lay my hands on my lap with palms facing up, and close my eyes. Today marks my third consecutive day of attempting meditation.

For beginners, the meditation gurus suggest focusing on your breath to quiet the mind. As I concentrate on the breath, I thought about whether the room smelled like cologne or fabric softener? I think it's cologne on a folded shirt from the night before. So again, I refocus on my breath. Thoughts cross my mind, and the more I tell myself not to interact with the thoughts, the more I think about the thoughts. So again, I refocus on my breath, and the mind finally quiets.

> *Thoughts emerge, but this time I notice and observe the thoughts without interacting with them as encouraged by Master Yogis. As I become mentally still, I feel at ease. If I focus too much on feeling at ease, then I create a thought and move out from the mental space of nothingness. I am not thinking about anything, but it feels like I should think about something. As I let go of control over my thoughts and focus on breath, the parade of thoughts and images fade. At last, a state of calmness. I can hear the air conditioner humming on low through the vents from above and notice the cool air tapping my left shoulder. My breath eases, and my mind is not focusing on anything. It reminds me of when we are thinking about the next word to say in a conversation and go completely blank. Except this time, going blank is the intention.*
>
> *I sit in this silent state for what I would consider a respectable amount of time. After some time has passed, I express gratitude. A feeling of joy and peace swells from within me. I close out my thoughts with a brief prayer, then still the mind again by focusing on the breath. With a clear mind, I sit in silence and feel the room. I slowly open my eyes. I look over at the clock, and it says 5:40. It felt like I was meditating for twenty minutes when it was seven minutes. As with most things in life, quality matters more than quantity. I feel emotionally and mentally free and motivated to embrace the day.*

My initial experiences with meditation are probably similar to your first attempts: mentally frustrating. Effective meditation occurs by developing the skills of focus and letting the thought go.

Meditation trains the mind to be silent and still. By doing so, we can achieve a heightened level of self-awareness. Through self-awareness of the present, we position ourselves for emotional calmness and mental clarity. Some people prefer guided meditation where an instructor leads focus through the meditation session, which can be just as beneficial as meditating unassisted. As long as we can achieve a state of calmness and emotional well-being, guided or not, it doesn't matter how we get there.

Meditating and visualizing in the morning is best since we can start our day at a higher vibrational frequency and be more mindful, which provides a positive foundation for a perfect day.

Meditation has become more popular than ever before. With all of the day-to-day activities that compete for our attention—work, family, cell phones, social media, and exercise—meditation can lower stress. Meditation as a daily activity provides a dedicated opportunity to immerse ourselves in silence and stillness and cleanse our subconscious to achieve valuable emotional and mental benefits in a relatively short period. Meditation is a form of mental hygiene and can improve your cognitive abilities. The effects of meditation can come quickly and help us make better day-to-day decisions as the sessions become effective.

Successful meditation requires practice and consistency. The ability to redirect thoughts, be in the present moment, and focus on nothing are skills we develop with intentional practice. Mind-wandering is the challenge many of us beginners experience. Beginners become meditation masters by trusting the process and intentionally practicing. Mantras such as "Om" from the ancient India Sanskrit language quiet the mind and shift consciousness as thoughts appear. Committing to the practice of meditation and improving the ability to observe breath and thoughts invites positive results. Meditation is not a practice to control the mind but to allow the mind to rest, recharge, and let be.

Recenter the mind by becoming clear and mindfully present. Meditation provides the perfect cognitive environment to release mental burdens and connect with your spiritual connection. I express gratitude with every meditation session, which raises vibrational energy and reinforces an abundant mindset before starting the day. Meditation and manifestation practices complement each other, wherein manifestation connecting to a spiritual connection from a calm and focused place is necessary for the request to be received. Manifesting or praying in an environment where we are distracted or disrupted is not practical. Meditation creates the space and conditions for clear thought and communication to occur. Over time, meditation can become habit-forming as you experience the benefits and the practice becomes part of your daily routine.

We can complete sessions anywhere we can achieve mental silence and stillness. I have meditated in the backseat of Ubers and taxis on the way to speaking engagements. For busy moms, meditation time may work best when scheduled as part of a daily to-do list. Mothers tend to be familiar with the sleep and activity patterns of their children and can plan accordingly. Meditating next to a sleeping baby can be most satisfying since there should be no infiltrating thoughts of what the baby is doing. Meditation schedules change, even for those without children, so be flexible and realize that some meditation sessions can be short depending on the day's activities or disturbances.

Meditation provides an opportunity to declutter the subconscious mind and practice mindfulness. Prioritizing a mental health activity can make a noticeable difference in how we feel and focus on tasks ahead, no matter how long or short. Mental clarity positions our beliefs and thoughts to evolve. We become empowered to view our perceived realities with calmness and responsiveness.

MINDFULLY MEDITATING

Meditation provides several health benefits. It helps eliminate stress, relieve lower back pain, improve memory and concentration, increase libido, and aid in better sleep—just to name a few.[7] With so many positive outcomes, it's no wonder millions of people all around the world meditate. Also, there are plenty of meditation apps to assist you, such as:

- Calm
- Headspace
- Insight Timer
- Smiling Mind
- Stop, Breathe & Think

As you follow the steps below toward your meditation journey, keep the ultimate goal in mind: peace.

1. Secure a place to be undisturbed for a desired amount of time.

"Undisturbed" in this sense does not mean there is nothing going on around you. It simply means that you are not physically or mentally disturbed. Many of us prefer a quiet room, study, or bedroom to meditate. Often, we are not at home or have access to a tranquil location, so we may have to be creative and resourceful to pull-off an impromptu meditation session. If we procrastinate or wait for perfect meditation conditions, we limit progress and positive outcomes.

So how can we fit meditation into our daily schedules? By meditating anywhere, we can comfortably sit for a while and achieve mental space to focus and breathe. Places that work well for meditating are patios, gardens, parks or lobbies, near fountains, benches, or sitting in a car or on a bus. My parents sit on the veranda, mentally silent and still,

7 *The Good Body*, "50 Mind-Blowing Meditation Facts You Need to Know!" last updated August 18, 2019, https://www.thegoodbody.com/meditation-facts/.

focused on nothing, and listening to the many sounds of nature. If you have the time and can achieve intentional focus in the space where you are, you can meditate.

2. Sit cross-legged on a floor or pillow with spine erect with hands on your lap and palms facing up.

For my yogis, sit in a lotus or half-lotus pose. If you are like me and flexibility is just not your thing, sit in a chair with your spine erect, feet firmly on the floor, and position your hands as you would sit cross-legged. Sometimes meditation positions may feel uncomfortable and detract from your focus. At a minimum, sit with a meditation posture with your torso positioned perpendicular to the floor. Achieving this posturing aligns your chakras to allow energy to flow.

3. Close your eyes or not.

Some of us prefer to stare or observe without concentrating on any object. That works too.

4. Become one with your breath.

Start with two or three deep breaths, then ease into a natural breathing pattern until your inhales and exhales are effortless. Visualize the expansion and contraction of air passing in and out of your body.

5. Observe and release thoughts that enter your mind.

The more you tell yourself not to think, the more you think. Just *be,* and as your mind wanders, let the thoughts pass by without judging or interacting with a single thought. If you think about something, observe the thought and refocus on the breath. See the thoughts but let them go. The approach works well with practice. Think of your thoughts as a slide show that you're flipping through without focusing on any individual slide. You see the slides, but you're disconnected from the details. Acknowledge your thoughts and let them be. Do not suppress thoughts—they will come back.

6. Scan the physical body mentally.
Feel your hands gently resting on your lap, feet resting on the floor, and the air ever so softly grazing your skin. Doing so diverts focus from your thoughts and expands self-awareness.

Practices such as meditation allow us to access the subconscious mind. We can create space to reduce the mental noise and learn how to be intentional with our thoughts. Focusing mindfully on positive thoughts, visualization, or spiritual connection, we can positively impact the subconscious mind. Using meditation becomes one of our many capabilities to create space to let go of negativity and reinforce limitless beliefs. Many successful people such as Clint Eastwood, Kendrick Lamar, Russell Brand, Tracee Ellis Ross, and Will Smith practice meditation.

Meditation should not be a burden or a chore. If we head into a meditation session with negative thoughts, we taint the experience and limit its effectiveness. Meditation becomes enjoyable as we master being mindful and reaping the benefits. Every part of us needs to rest, especially our minds, to perform at optimal levels. The feeling of clarity that accompanies a lighter mind brings us back for mental maintenance session after session. The steps for a relaxing meditation session are minimal and do not require special tools or equipment.

Why doesn't everybody meditate? The drawbacks that deter the adoption of meditation practices are that meditation takes time, focus to still the mind, and negative feelings or thoughts can resurface. For an alternative, several everyday activities can be equally effective. Going for a walk, practicing yoga, resting, cleaning a house, journaling, coloring in a coloring book, or listening to music are just a few activities that can be effective if we're mindfully present as we execute the activity.

Often, we overlook our mental health. If we can become proficient in clearing our thoughts and regaining focus, the benefits of meditation will outweigh any potential drawbacks. Practicing mental hygiene creates space for our minds to function healthily, as intended. Instead of hitting the snooze button on the alarm clock, use the nine minutes to meditate before getting ready for the day. If setting aside five minutes for meditation before heading out the door works better, then do that. Suppose morning rituals are not your thing. Set aside time in the afternoon for meditation. Maybe meditating just before bed works best for you—then do that. There are twenty-four hours in a day, and five to ten minutes is all it takes for meditation to impact your day. You are worth it!

We need a mental break from our lives and a few minutes of complete focus on nothingness can go a long way for our mind, body, and spirit. There are resources available online from various providers that introduce different meditation practices that fit your needs. Find something about meditation that interests you and go with it. If a comfy meditation outfit, favorite meditating room, or relaxing fragrant candle gets you in the meditation mood, then go for it!

Be consistent, trust the process, and feel the difference. You will find creative ways to secure a meditation session even if the conditions are not perfect. Just a few minutes for focus, mindfulness, and clarity can offset a full day of disturbances and disruptions. The power is yours to create a reality of mental, emotional, and physical wellness.

TIME FOR REFLECTION

I intend to learn more about the meditation practices by

I intend to meditate in the morning, afternoon, evening [circle one].

I intend to practice my meditation at:

I intend to meditate for ____________ minutes ____________ times a week.

CHAPTER ELEVEN

Time Travel Is Overrated

"Realize deeply that the present moment is all you have. Make the NOW the primary focus of your life."
—Eckhart Tolle

ONE DECEMBER MORNING, I flew back to St. Louis, where ten inches of snow layered the city, the average temperature was 17 degrees, and I did not have a hat. Hats matter more in colder climates when less hair grows on top of our heads. During the flight and most of the evening, I mulled over past experiences, decisions, and relationships. I was entering into an uncharted chapter of my life in search of happiness and purpose. My energy differed from the confident and secure vibes of the past. I felt depressed about how I got here and anxious about where I was going.

That night, I couldn't sleep as my mind welcomed thought after thought and I felt like I was coming down with a cold. I was miserable! At daybreak, I felt the urge to be anywhere tropically warm to unplug and regain health, peace, and clarity.

I connected with a colleague for dinner that evening and shared thoughts of traveling, solo, for the Christmas holiday season. My colleague was married and a mother with two children under age five. She seemed more excited about my tentative plans than I was and ready to live vicariously through my intentions as I pondered this trip. We discussed destination possibilities, shared travel experiences, and concluded our travel destination review with Belize. I had never been there, and after weighing the destination against other options, Belize seemed perfect for a personal retreat.

After returning to Charlotte, I packed my bags, purchased a GoPro camera, and headed back to the airport a few days later. It took longer to pack for paradise than expected, and I missed the flight. With positive thoughts and exchanging kind words with the airline staff, they offered an evening flight to Miami, Florida, and a next-day flight to Belize. I said, "I'll take it!" Two tropical destinations on one trip. The staff had assigned an exit row seat, a leg and a half away from the flight attendant's jump seat. During takeoff, I met the flight attendant, a Panamanian from Nebraska that lived in Charlotte. We chatted about the books we were reading, her knowledge of Belize and exchanged a story or two.

After arriving at my last-minute Airbnb in Miami, I showered and headed out to an eclectic part of Miami with art galleries, plenty of locals, and ethnic restaurants. The evening was amazing: clear sky, great music, flavorful food, and talkative people. I winded down the evening at a music lounge with a pair of Peruvian sisters who taught me Bachata and Merengue dance moves. Pretty cool experience considering that Miami was not in the original travel itinerary. Maybe Miami was part of a grander plan. Every moment felt natural and expected.

The following day, I headed to the airport and began recording the trip. I had "tourist" written all over me with a video camera in hand. I was there for it all. The airline delayed my late morning flight for a couple of hours, so I explored the airport for lunch. I encountered a woman heading in the same direction, so we chatted it up while looking for a place to eat. She was from Belize, traveling alone and heading to see her family for the holidays.

We had lunch, and she filled me in on Belizean places to explore and things to expect. I was grateful for her insights and guidance.

I arrived in Belize in the late evening exhausted from the travel. My vacation condo was on a twenty-five-mile island, Ambergris Caye, where a golf cart is the primary form of transportation. I didn't have a golf cart, so I walked a block to a restaurant to have a meal. A gentleman named Oliver from the United Kingdom sat next to me at the bar. We greeted and chatted about my travels to Belize and his life. Oliver retired from his job at forty-eight and used an inheritance to travel to vacation destinations year-round. As I listened to his lifestyle, I became envious. Who wouldn't want to go to different destinations across the globe every two weeks? The more he shared, and the more I reflected on his words and what he *wasn't* saying, the more I realized he was unhappy and searching for his purpose. Coincidence? I wanted to say, "Oliver, you're searching all over the world for happiness and purpose, and you're not going to find it!" Of course, I didn't say that. Instead, I yawned, shook hands, and went back to the condo.

I woke up in the morning with intentions to relax and enjoy a full day of downtime—a notion that lasted for two hours and seventeen minutes. Who was I kidding? I like thrills and frills while on vacation, so I explored the island, rented a golf cart, and signed up for a few excursions.

Local business owners greeted me with open arms and offered advice on tourist traps and hidden-gem restaurants. I met an older Jamaican restaurant owner, Donovan, that moved to Belize many years ago to marry his Belizean girlfriend. We shared stories, he quizzed me on the Jamaican knowledge handed down from my parents, and we discussed the beauty of Belize. High vibrations and memorable experiences filled the next few days. I went snorkeling, and cave-tubing, spectated a hermit crab race and chicken drop Bingo and climbed Mayan Ruins.

During the Mayan Ruins tour, I met Hank, a sixty-year-old solo traveler who was a Chicago inner-city educator. Hank and I struck up a conversation as we waited for others to join the tour. Hank did not know the struggles I carried leaving the US but began revealing his journey like a grandfather sharing wisdom with a grandson. There was a lesson in every sentence he spoke. Hank shared guidance on dwelling on the past and attempting to control the future and drew me into his stories with his coarse voice and clear-sighted eyes. I intently listened and mirrored his breath, giving him confidence that his words were heard as he divulged more and more.

Hank had been living his life mindfully and with a purpose for the last twenty-plus years, but it wasn't always so. He made a con-scious choice to be passionate and intentional about his happiness after falling into a bottomless emotional rut chasing meaningless gratification. Although the experiences that connected Hank and me were different, the constant restlessness and search for peace were the same. Coincidence? His stories echoed feelings and thoughts that festered within me for years. I walked away from the experience with a sense that God was trying to tell me something or point me in a direction.

The next day, I met a divorcée from San Francisco who often traveled solo and collected art. I met a local business owner from Charleston, South Carolina, who moved to Belize on a whim. On my last day in the country, I met a Jamaican taxi driver on the way to the airport. He played roots reggae music that reminded me of my childhood with my parents. Coincidence? The driver and I shared stories as we appreciated familiar songs and artists. I realized just how impactful the trip had become. Every encounter and conversation were refreshing and had meaning.

I stayed in Belize for seven days, and the trip ended just as fast as it had begun. I practiced meditation and self-reflection daily and returned home feeling self-aware and calm. I settled back into my daily routines and connected with my emotions and thoughts like never before. My vibrational energy was higher than in recent years. My mind was still and silent. The cycling of negative thoughts of yesterday was not there. My fears about the future had vanished. As I watched the recorded footage from the trip and thought about every interaction and conversation, I felt emotional as I watched myself on camera. I wasn't sure when it started, but a mindset evolution was taking place. The sequence of events and people I engaged with during the trip were intricate parts of a spontaneous journey of growth. The trip to St. Louis had sparked a chain reaction of events that led to this mindful moment of clarity.

We are the creators of our reality, after all.

Every disruption from the moment I left Charlotte for St. Louis did not happen by chance. Everything happened with purpose *for me.* Sometimes we place challenges and obstacles before ourselves to direct us to a better path.

If I had brought a hat to St. Louis, would I have been miserable enough for a pricey last-minute getaway to a tropical paradise? If I hadn't missed the original flight to Belize, would I have met the Panamanian flight attendant, the Peruvian sisters, and the Belizean native in Miami? The flight snafus, dancing in Miami, daring island excursions, unlikely conversations and life-changing experiences happened because of the intention to regain my health, peace, and clarity.

The travel plans for Belize were flexible and invited experiences to come to me. Nothing was forced, controlled, or manipulated. I was mindful, living in the now, engaged in every moment, and invited people into my life who added value. Everyone from the colleague in St. Louis to the South Carolina ex-pat in Belize served me in ways that inspired clarity, perspective, and growth.

The conversation with Oliver uncovered an external search for happiness and purpose. The Jamaican restaurant owner, Donovan, brought me back to a mental place where I was happiest: "Country"—my Dad's childhood home. Hank showed me we have everything in us to evolve our mindset to one of abundance. The traveling divorcée and ex-pat business owner showed me what it means to re-discover your happiness and purpose. We discover peace for ourselves. A spontaneous solo trip to Belize has become one of my top three most life-changing experiences. I am indeed a believer in living mindfully and launching intentional experiences!

In such a fast-paced society full of distractions and disruptions, many of us make reactionary decisions, seek happiness externally, and worry about obstacles or concerns that have not come into existence. Reactionary decisions or outcomes lead to mistakes or regret and create conditions that invite depression. Worries generate fear and anxiety. Reaching for happiness leads to mental and physical attachments that drive us to abandon ourselves. Are you reaching for happiness?

We cannot control the past or the future, but we can control ourselves in the present. The past was the present, and the future will be the present. By practicing mindfulness—being consciously aware, we can master our emotions, thoughts, and actions and invite intentional outcomes into our life. We are making the conscious choice to be nonjudgmental and aware of our feelings, thoughts, and actions in the present moment.

How are you living your life today? Are you sacrificing the present by dwelling on the past or being focused on the future? Mental time travel does more harm than good. Do you fear the future or losing people? Being mindful is a way of living and ability we all possess but take for granted. We rarely use mindfulness to its full extent. Mindfulness is another superpower (visualization is the other) that we as human beings forget we have.

Living present allows us to embrace curiosity and consciously remove negativity from ourselves and toward others. With mindfulness, we're able to respond to anything with connectedness and in control of our emotions and thoughts. We associate this concept with neuroplasticity—the brain's ability to address life situations and circumstances as our emotions, thoughts, and actions change. Establishing a success mindset unleashes limitless beliefs. We expand our perceived realities with positive thoughts that replace negative views of the past and concerns for the future. The Greek philosopher Aristotle notes, "Knowing yourself is the beginning of all wisdom." Practicing mindfulness enhances the brain's ability to respond to situations or circumstances objectively. We can develop an emotional intelligence to express, manage, and be attentive to how we feel and behave.

Right now, at this moment, we have no concerns or worry if we are mindfully present. The past should not affect your engagement with this book chapter. Dwelling on the previous chapter or worrying about the next chapter should not change your connection with this chapter. You have control over your mental presence and actionable responses right now. Why worry about what you cannot control, the past and future? Fully engaging with this chapter without shame, resentment, or judgment provides a chance to discover an encouraging outlook and invite positive experiences. Intentionally immersing yourself in this chapter prepares you for the next chapter. Do you see what I did there? Are we still talking about chapters of this book? Or are we talking about chapters of your life? At this moment, we notice the deep black color of the printed words, the texture of the pages, and the weight of the book in our hands. We are consciously aware of how we are digesting the information and feel connected to each thought. At last, the beauty of mindfulness!

Many of us multitask—share brain space between functions to complete more than one task simultaneously. Multitasking depletes productivity, which is the quality and awareness of each task. It is scientifically not possibly to deliver our highest value to a task if we are multitasking. A study by Professor Earl K. Miller at the Massachusetts Institute of Technology (MIT found that multitasking reduces productivity by 40 percent or more and contributes to the release of stress hormones in the body.[8] We negatively impact our bodies and limit successful outcomes when we multitask.

How less stressful would a morning commute be if we were not on the cell phone, swearing at drivers, or speeding through traffic? What if, instead, we observe the trees, rolling hills, and architecture of buildings as we rest our minds and enjoy the ride? Red stoplights would have a different meaning. An impatient wait for the green light becomes the freedom to explore and connect with our emotions and mental space. Every moment of the drive becomes satisfying. We discover things and places that we pass mindlessly and see ourselves in ways that typically go unnoticed. We arrive at work in peace, ready to start the workday with patience and optimism. Our vibrational energy and levels of self-awareness are higher, inviting positivity into our day.

Let's compare this mindful commute to one where we're on the cell phone, swearing at drivers, speeding through traffic, and late for work. We curse at the driver who just cut us off or react with the finger while nearly rear-ending the vehicle in front of us. We speed as gaps between cars appear, even though we get as far as the older gentleman who gracefully obeys the speed limit. We veer onto the shoulder as we try to send the text message, "Running late."

Sound familiar?

---

8 Chen, Amy. "Why Multitasking Is Blocking Your Path to Success." Entrepreneur, May 31, 2019. https://www.entrepreneur.com/article/334609.

Consider the number of reactionary decisions on your commute. Multiply the number of reactionary choices by the number of drivers that are on the road each day. That's a considerable number! By speeding, we are attempting to change our lateness, the past, and the time we arrive at work, the future. Why else would we be speeding through traffic?

Let's consider the negativity and unfavorable outcomes we invite into our day well before stepping into the office after such a commute. As we arrive late to the office, we spill our second cup of coffee, have a tense discussion with our boss, and cancel items on our to-do list to redo tasks we hastily completed. Our emotions, thoughts, and actions have created a negative reality.

Suppose multiple drivers had a lousy morning and are inviting negativity in their day by their thoughts and actions. The result is a high number of people with low vibrational energy having bad days. No wonder stress is everywhere! Everything, no matter how insignificant, contributes negatively or positively to the chain of actions that create our reality. We witnessed a positive chain of actions that led to correlated outcomes with my trip to Belize.

As I detached myself from negative emotions and thoughts and triggered intentional actions, I unleashed health, peace, and clarity into my life. Why not create a reality that unleashes intentional success? The results can be limitless. Dad always says, "Pay attention to what you are doing." I was always thinking about or doing multiple things sparking unfavorable consequences during the earlier years of my life. Dad is not a monk, psychic, or spiritual leader, but he knows positive outcomes are likely with focus. Mindfulness is simply paying attention with intention. Live every day mindfully, and you can create your best reality.

LIVING A MINDFUL LIFE

You can develop a lifestyle that repels negativity and invites positivity through your thought patterns and intentional habits. By practicing mindfulness, you're able to create and discover meaningful happenings of joy and satisfaction. There are several key steps to develop a mindful state.

1. Be in the moment.

Allow yourself to be present in the *now*. Look around you, and what do you see? Focus on an object without touching it, and describe the object to yourself in no less than five minutes. Be descriptive, as if you were trying to sell the object to yourself. You realize quickly that it's impossible to describe the object *and* think about what you ate for lunch yesterday. As you describe the components of the object, assess how the colors make you feel. Is the object hard or soft? What are you thinking?

If you're having difficulties connecting with this exercise, close your eyes, focus on your breathing, and try again. Practice wherever you would like. When I'm on a treadmill, it doesn't take long for negative thoughts such as "I'm tired" or "I'm bored" to appear. Non-motivating thoughts do not help fitness goals. When I shift focus to enjoying the atmosphere, noting the good things about my form, and reciting inspiring affirmations, I become no longer tired or bored and complete the workout. Mindfulness leads to focus, and focus leads to successful results.

2. Listen beyond hearing.

We are all guilty of multitasking while listening to others. Often, we give physical and verbal cues that we are listening but are daydreaming. Mindful listening is to be aware and not let judgments, beliefs, emotions, or unrelated thoughts supersede the communication process. As someone is communicating, we should be engaged to understand everything that is being communicated. If we are not engaged, why listen at all?

Use active listening techniques like paraphrasing and mirroring to enable you to connect and remain present authentically. The conversation and rapport will be meaningful for both parties. We saw this in the talk with Hank. If random thoughts appear during the dialogue, briefly focus on breath, observe the thought, and reengage into the conversation. With practice, mindful listening becomes natural and informative and brings more enjoyment to the art of conversation and listening.

3. Focus on one task at a time.

Multitasking may seem like an ideal way of doing things. We may feel productive, but *are* we productive? We can think we're multitasking, but the brain can only execute one task at a time. Those of us who multitask have a hard time focusing on a single task. The brain switches from task to task and information escapes. Studies by the Harvard Business Review show that multitasking shrinks brain gray matter, intelligence, and lowers IQ.[9]

Let's compare the brain's task-switching ability to the likeness of feeding a cranky and agitated pair of two-year-old twin babies at the same time. Picture two distracted babies sitting side by side, and as we send two spoonsful, one in each hand, of tasty veggie puree their way, more of the food falls on their clothes than in their mouths. We can increase productivity by focusing on sending a spoonful to one baby at a time. The scenario is the same for the brain. By focusing on a single task, or *mindful*-tasking, and engaging with the task at hand, the brain optimally processes the information.

Daily planners, to-do lists, habit trackers, and goal planners are great at helping us complete personal or professional tasks. They enable us to be more productive, save time, and preserve intelligence. Several productivity apps can be helpful with mindful-tasking:

9 Peter Bregman, "How (and Why) to Stop Multitasking," Harvard Business Review, May 20, 2010, https://hbr.org/2010/05/how-and-why-to-stop-multitaski.

- 24me — Intuitive virtual assistant
- Daily Planner — Habit tracker
- Fabulous — Goal planner and tracker
- Google Tasks — Task manager
- MinimaList — To-do list manager

Planning your day into task-oriented time slots helps with concentration and stress and saves time. Schedule dedicated time to be on the phone, check emails or connect with family. Minimize distractions and disruptions, and carry out tasks to the best of your ability. Your phone calls will be more interactive, the total time to check emails will be less, and your email responses will be complete. Your family will be grateful and appreciate having your undivided attention. You are more effective at completing anything with quality when you put your mind to it!

4. Respond, not react to negativity.

Life presents plenty of situations and circumstances that create resistance and invite negativity. But we are in control of how negativity affects us. By being intentional with our emotions and thoughts, we can influence the outcome's narrative with our response. We should not dwell on or suppress negative emotions but acknowledge and feel them. Emotions alert us to know what feels right and wrong. The goal here is to go through what we need to learn, grow, and move forward with strength and wisdom toward a solution. Being mindfully aware of how you're feeling provides space to respond.

Journaling and other self-care methods supplement space to help us work through negative emotions. Start focusing on the breath to increase awareness, mentally step back from the situation, and let go of what you cannot control. Whether you're having a bad day or enduring a tragic event or tragedy, take a moment to consider what you're grateful for and what's going right. Dwelling on the concern attaches us to blame, resentment, and judgment. Align your thoughts and actions with your values and transition energy away from the problem to the solution. Everyone heals in their own time, but you have complete control of how the healing affects your actions and outcomes. Meditate, exercise, or do something that gives you a moment to reset before responding or addressing the situation.

Mindfulness is a simple concept for some of us and a tall order for others. With repetition and living moment to moment, mindfulness can become an enjoyable way of life. We often focus on what's in front of us and miss the bigger picture. The benefits of mindfulness are unlimited once we master tuning into the mind and body and living in the present. Benefits include increased brain gray matter, less stress, lower blood pressure, greater concentration, reduced anxiety, better sleep, and the list goes on. Slowing down our daily lives enough to observe, feel, and think in every moment can make a difference in our health, well-being, and overall happiness. Shifting our mindset from reactionary to a responsive state reduces the impact of our negative emotions. Mindful thoughts and actions take us through life's trials and tribulations with an intentional presence and provide an authentic understanding of ourselves.

TIME FOR REFLECTION

I intend to learn to be present, starting with:

I intend to be an active listener by:

Instead of multitasking, I intend to practice time blocking, using:

When negative things occur, I intend to respond by:

CHAPTER TWELVE

The Art of Chaos Coordination

"The first step in crafting the life you want is to get rid of everything you don't."
—Joshua Becker

THE BENEFITS OF decluttering go beyond reducing and reorganizing our material possessions. Decluttering can apply to the mind to create space and unleash better outcomes. We can minimize or eliminate anything that does not add value to our lives. We must make room for happiness and success.

Clutter stagnates vibrational energy, invites chaos, and leads to procrastination and indecisive thoughts and actions. Decluttering is a form of self-care and supports wellness. Our energy, thoughts, and actions must align with our intentions to make our goals a reality. How can intentional focus exist with clutter? Clutter invites distractions and disruptions, which dilute focus and delay or stalls progress. Living a chaotic life in any form blocks abundance.

If we are seeking intentional relationships with people, we should live our life intentionally. An intentional life attracts an intentional life. Alternatively, drama attracts drama. As human beings, we struggle with matters of the heart and hold on to confusion and disorder with our relationships. Are friends *really* friends? Do we tolerate people for companionship? Do relationships align with our values? Relationships that do not feel healthy or invite happiness are clutter. Purposeful space enables us to flourish. Intentional success occurs when we prepare our lives for what we want and project the values we wish to receive. Let go of negative people and embrace the relationships that add value to your life. Decluttering relationships and setting intentions create room for authentic connections to thrive.

The concept of decluttering is often forgotten when planning and pursuing goals. Decluttering helps us prepare to receive. Clutter affects mindfulness and our efforts to live purposeful lives since distractions and disruptions limit our ability to receive and succeed. The more distractions and disruptions we can minimize, the greater our perceived reality can become. Would your consumption and understanding of information improve without distraction and disruption? There is power in applying mindfulness to all areas of our lives.

Decluttering and goals go together like peanut butter and jelly. Recall that focused energy, feelings, and thoughts create opportunities and spur actions for intentional success. If we're overcrowding the mind with doubt and unrelated thoughts, achieving our goals will be difficult and unsuccessful. Applying for jobs that misalign with our values or goals creates distractions and disruptions and obstructs progress toward the job we want. When we're applying for jobs just to see what happens, we're exuding doubt with every application that is not in alignment with our goals. How many random job inquiries turn into desirable offers? If we are honest, a few. A better approach is to declutter the job search to create space and focus on the jobs that align with your intentions.

The subconscious mind's programming contains innate beliefs that enforce the idea that more is better—a mental composition for survival. We want more juice, more food, more candy, more presents, more toys, more friends, more education, more money, more everything, and thus, more happiness. Wait. Does "more" of anything equal happiness?

For some of us, more money means we clutter our lives with our labor's souvenirs to show our success. We purchase excessive material possessions because we can. The desire to have more money matters less than the intention for wanting more money. As Dr. Wayne Dyer often said, "Everything begins with intention." Many of us want to earn more money. When we want to earn more money, we're in a scarcity mindset. All of our thoughts and actions that follow reflect want and lack once we have more money. We clutter our lives with things we don't need for fear of missing out on the latest and greatest or because we're attached to others' opinions or expectations. Instead, have a success mindset and consider how we can deliver more value to earn more money. The more value you provide, the more people are willing to pay you, whether it is management, consumers, or clients. When we focus on delivering value to earn more money, we spend money with a success mindset, as if we already have everything we need and want.

Taking on more responsibility, being more innovative, offering better products, enhancing your services, and increasing your skills are ways to add value. More value positions us for more excellent opportunities that can monetarily reward our lives. Intentions set with a success mindset positively influence our thoughts and actions that follow. Success is not in earning money or the clutter we purchase, *but in the value delivered.*

Maintaining less financial clutter with necessity spending and debt allows us to save and build wealth to create the lives we desire. Old-school financial wisdom holds true today as it has for centuries, "Save for a rainy day," or as Mom used to say, "Don't hang your hat where you can't reach it."

Do you recall the onset of the pandemic and its effect on employment and businesses? Millions of people suddenly found themselves unable to work or unemployed. Saving and building wealth begins with decluttering our financial lives. When we minimize unnecessary spending and reallocate the funds to pay off debt, we create space for income accumulation through saving and productive uses for money. Detach from earning the next dollar, others' opinions and expectations, the next best thing, and minimize clutter. An uncluttered life is a happy life.

The concept of decluttering applies to living a healthy lifestyle as well! We can create space to make it easier to live healthier. Eating healthy can be a challenge when sugary or processed foods are in reach instead of healthy and nutritional foods. Create space for healthy foods by removing junk foods and restocking cabinets and the refrigerator with healthy foods. Toss out the bad stuff and replace it with the good stuff. The next time you reach for a snack or make a dish, only healthy items will be available. Our bodies feel better, and our brains can function better with healthy food. Make nutritional changes over time and create a healthy lifestyle that you're able to sustain. If you love pizza with extra cheese, don't omit pizza with extra cheese from your life. Be intentional about what you eat, the amount you eat, and how often you eat it. Everything in life works best with intention and moderation. Diets do not add long-term value, but nutritional lifestyle changes can!

DECLUTTERING YOUR LIFE

Decluttering, as you've seen, can apply to multiple areas in life: career, relationships, health, finances—the sky is the limit with creating room for everything you want. Come back to these steps and apply them to as many areas as needed.

1. Organize your intentions.

Intentions bring focus to an objective, task, or goal. Our intentions must be simple and position us to allocate energy, thought, and action toward executing and achieving the intended outcome. Organizing intentions allows us to be more precise with what we want and focus on purpose.

Write a set of intentions for career, relationships, health, and finances that align with happiness and success. Consider each intent and gauge how the meaning affiliates with your values. For example, an intention for your career could be "I intend to be productive with my business," which aligns with your commitment and reliability values. Organize your intentions by category, career, relationships, health, and finances, and consider why each intention is essential to you. Don't dwell on the outcome of carrying out the intention.

2. Make a declutter checklist.

Lists can be great for minimizing clutter! Write items, people, and habits you should let go of to align with your intentions. Don't think, just write. For example, decluttering may include letting go of frequent breaks or surfing the internet to accomplish more tasks. To drink more water every day may mean letting go of juice and soda. To have relationships that do not stress you may include letting go of negative people. Increasing your monthly savings may involve letting go of spending on meals that you can prepare at home.

Organize in a checklist manner that makes it easy to assess the tasks to declutter your life. Any item, person, or habit that no longer brings you joy should be on the list. Anything or anyone without purpose or value in your life distracts and disrupts your intentions. Write all clutter on the list.

3. Start decluttering simply.

Begin decluttering your life by starting small. Start with items, people, and habits that are easy wins or simple to let go. Daily decluttering habits gain momentum as you become comfortable with needing and wanting less. Doing something small each day adds up to completing larger tasks on your list. The more serious and restrictive you are about what you let and keep in your life, the more impactful decluttering becomes. Think like a minimalist, keep what you need, and get rid of anything that does not serve you, including people.

Many of us do not consider people when we think about decluttering. Surrounding yourself with toxic people or people who negatively affect you can confine your thoughts and actions, limiting your happiness and success. Pessimists, complainers, whiners, and victims can impede our emotions, cause stress, and lower confidence in ourselves. Decluttering people begins with detaching from relationships that do not align with your values or cause frustration. Redirect energy, thoughts, and actions toward people that encourage and support you and have your best interests in mind. As you align your relationships and communities with your values, the relationships that do not add to your life starve and falter as your energy toward those relationships decreases.

As you move through the declutter checklist, you feel lighter and see the space you're creating to invite what you want into your life. Think of your cluttered life as a home, and you're creating space for permanent guests who bring happiness. The pleasing visual result, feelings of accomplishment, and overall joy will motivate you to do more and declutter elsewhere. Don't attempt to declutter your whole "house" in a single day. If you do, decluttering your life will feel like a enormous chore and progress will stall.

As you focus and feel the shift in vibrational energy, celebrate and move on to other areas. When decluttering your home and sticking with a minimalistic mindset, you'll notice that your life is inherently improving. Let go and detach from all that does not excite you, and feel ample space inviting a refined sense of joy and success into your life.

3. Finish what you start.

If you can see yourself getting started, you can see yourself finishing. Finishing whatever you start maintains momentum, embraces accomplishment, and inspires you to take on even more. This concept sounds simple, but many of us start more endeavors than we can finish. Starting small and completing each decluttering opportunity leads to a manageable pace. We position ourselves, with every small decluttering accomplishment, to achieve the end goal of having a decluttered life.

4. Become organized.

Creating a designated place for everything in your life is essential to ensuring your life remains decluttered. There's a time and a place for everything and everyone. If something or someone seems out of place in your life, they probably are. Organizers, planners, and trackers can be a great way to organize.

We overlook decluttering our lives as we realize our potential and pursue success. When our container is full, we can no longer receive. Decluttering our lives empties our containers to receive our goals and achieve success. There is no room for guests when you have a crowded house. The fewer distractions and disruptions, the more space in your life for happiness and success to enter and remain. Clutter drains energy and provides no value to our peace and contentment. By decluttering, we transform the energy that hinders our progress into energy that flows and propels our progress.

TIME FOR REFLECTION

I intend to declutter my life starting with these three areas:

Here are three ways I can become more organized in my life:

I intend to maintain a decluttered life by:

PART III
Change Your Life

CHAPTER THIRTEEN

Win with the Love of the Dream

"Don't chase the paper, chase the dream."
—Sean Combs

BEFORE MY SENIOR year in high school, I left a cushy job at a dollar store in the mall to become a lot associate at a home improvement store. The new gig paid three dollars more per hour and provided management opportunities! More money, more happiness, right? New responsibilities included:

- Arriving to work at 6:00 p.m. on the weekdays and 7:00 a.m. on the weekends.
- Retrieving lumber and shopping carts.
- Loading purchased goods into and onto vehicles.
- Driving a forklift (which was quite fun).
- Cleaning public restrooms and collecting store trash.

The additional income supported car payments and insurance and yielded financial independence. More money doesn't come without sacrifice. Attending Friday night football games, after-school events, and weekend gatherings didn't happen. Instead, I retrieved carts in wet and cold weather, got splinters and scrapes loading lumber and materials, and unclogged overflowing toilets. The appeal of earning more money disappeared as quickly as a shooting star.

Each workday was physically exhausting, but I was more bothered by working on weekends and holidays. I often thought about having a career with a 9-to-5 schedule, nights, holidays, and weekends off, in a climate-controlled environment. My mindset shifted toward my values and passions as I detached focus from money. My unwavering work ethic and willingness to go above and beyond the call of duty grabbed management's attention. I developed strategies to network with store department leaders and increase my product knowledge of one or two departments. I gained product knowledge through self-paced courses during downtime and lunch breaks. In less than six months, I ascended to a lumber and building materials sales associate.

As a sales associate, I enjoyed the customer interactions and being a go-to expert for lumber and building material products. The more I focused on adding value to my job and the customer experience, the more satisfied I became. A year later, I moved higher to become the assistant department head of building materials co-responsible for the department's inventory. My home improvement career was looking up, and I was making good money for a college student. But as I prepared for my third year of college, I returned from the U.S. Marine Officer Candidate School with a new perspective and growing interest in finance.

I interviewed for a check-processing position at a financial services company where I would remove staples from and taped ripped bank deposited checks. Nothing was exciting about check processing. The job paid far less than the assistant department head position, but it aligned with my intention to enter the world of finance. The interviewing HR recruiter seemed baffled by my interest in the position, "Why would you give up a management position and higher pay for a check-processing position?" I simply stated, "I am here for a career, not a job." Twenty-three years after being hired, I still work 9-to-5 in a climate-controlled environment with nights, weekends, and holidays off, just like I had envisioned. I deliver value to the same financial services company except as a senior vice president in the investment management division. Dreams and visions can become reality!

Our most significant life lessons position us to deliver the most incredible amount of value once our mindset and actions align with our passions and goals, not money.

We force lifestyles that resemble our perceived definition of happiness and success when we attach our outcomes to money. We see this scenario often when we overextend ourselves with credit or deplete our bank accounts. From childhood through adolescence, we learn from and observe successful people. Perceived success becomes the car, house, and clothes successful people have. As a teenager, my perceived measure of happiness and success was paying for a car on my own and being financially free. Dad shared his childhood stories of living poor and dreaming of owning a two-story house with a white picket fence. It's the story that never gets old. A two-story house was his perceived measure of success.

What is your perceived measure of success?

Let's consider movies, music videos, corporate executives, business owners, successful doctors and lawyers, professional athletes, and musicians. We find their lifestyles consist of luxury cars, large houses, posh clothing, and expensive jewelry. As children matriculate through the education system, the lavish lifestyles of a small percentage of the world become the primary reason for many to consider career paths such as lawyers, doctors, engineers, and athletes. Our career aspirations drift from providing our highest value to society to pursuing high-income material items. This thought changes as we realize the amount of school required or that math, science, and history are not our favorite subjects. If we had aspirations of becoming an athlete, we realize that our athletic talent has limitations or our focus to compete at the college level has dwindled.

As we understand our strengths and weaknesses and become young adults, our career interests expand and align with roles that may not have the prestige or income of a doctor, lawyer, engineer, or athlete. Instead, we pursue careers such as counselor, teacher, or analyst. The appeal of luxury cars, large houses, posh clothing, and expensive jewelry hasn't changed but our career choices have. How do we achieve a high-income lifestyle without the patience or career path to take us there? We supplement income sources to create the lifestyle we desire through saving, investing, borrowing, marrying well, having multiple jobs, and juggling side hustles.

Some of us want to live a victorious lifestyle before earning it and seek opportunities to force outcomes. Forcing anything never works out well. Practicing patience and employing financially responsible behaviors lead to successful financial results.

When we have a scarcity mindset, we attach ourselves to the next dollar to hoard or spend. We've seen people with high-end luxury cars and houses, but live paycheck to paycheck. Others may live simply but attach themselves to money, never enjoying their affluence because of age, illness, death, or fear of the unknown. Practicing patience and employing financially responsible behaviors lead to successful financial results.

Self-sabotaging "money over everything" behavior is seated in fear, insecurities, and a desire to live up to others' expectations and opinions. Many of us purchase beyond our means for instant gratification, worldly success, or status approval. Some of us are hardwired to keep up with the Joneses or seek belongingness to a social or economic group. We can only rely on acronyms and phrases such as "YOLO" (You Only Live Once) or "carpe diem" (Latin for "seize the day") so many times to rationalize impulsive overspending before becoming financially depleted.

By focusing and acting based on our passions and aligning our thoughts and actions with a success mindset, the path to success opens, and money follows. Typically, the top 20 percent of people in any industry make roughly 80 percent of the capital. Why? The top 20 percent of people deliver value based on their passion and purpose, while the remaining 80 percent deliver value focused on the money. Ever wonder why musicians, actors, or athletes perform well after their peak of success? They're passionate about their craft and are living out their purpose. Having passion and a success mindset brings money their way.

Attracting and having money begins with being prudent and believing we can easily have money. If we're continually accumulating debt or overspending, we will invite higher debt levels and more spending obligations. Everything begins and ends with having the right mindset and replacing limiting beliefs. We can live comfortably and wealthy. Wealthy, in this case, is not only financially. Wealthy is happy and secure to live life pleasurably based on your perceived reality. Time is available to everyone. How we allocate time and focus determines the difference in how we live and achieve levels of success. If we spend time focusing on wanting money, we will receive more *want* than cash. If we spend time creating value through the activity or endeavor that leads us to money, our aligned passions and actions invite financial success. The dollars come to us when we abundantly live out our ambitions with intention.

INVITING MORE MONEY INTO YOUR LIFE

Many of us blame our early beginnings for our financial shortcomings. We're in control of changing the narrative of our perceived realities at any time. Howard Schultz, CEO of Starbucks, grew up in public housing. Do Won Chang, Forever 21 founder, worked as

10 G. William Domhoff, "Wealth, Income, and Power," *Who Rules America?* last updated April 2017, https://whorulesamerica.ucsc.edu/power/wealth.html.

a janitor and at a gas station. Ralph Lauren worked as a clerk for Brooks Brothers. You can invite money into your life by intentionally pursuing your passions and dreams.

1. Replace self-sabotaging beliefs and thoughts.

You can be financially successful regardless of your financial disposition. Do you have the mindset of a financially successful person or the mentality of the general masses? An intentional financial journey begins with letting go of jealousy, resentment, competitiveness, and the need for approval. We have to drop the rocks to swim to the top. Let go of negative, debilitating thoughts and beliefs and adopt a success mindset that focuses on contributing value instead of wasting money. Money does not create happiness. Happiness is created by advancing toward your goals. We maximize satisfaction and invite money into our lives when we align our values, beliefs, and actions with delivering our highest value.

A scarcity mindset attached to money creates limited results. To practice replacing the limiting belief of lack, thoughtfully consider the financial outcome you desire. Are you dreaming of becoming a millionaire in ten years? Live financially free in five years? The only person that limits your financial success is you. You may not believe you make enough money to be financially free. Is that a limiting belief? It is. Replace limiting beliefs with an intention, such as, "I intend to be financially free." What does financially free mean to you? Can you see yourself achieving financial success? Align your thoughts and actions with the belief of unlimited financial success.

We have to change our mindset and our actions to ingrain greater possibilities and expand the subconscious mind's beliefs. Align your thoughts, actions, and lifestyle with your financial goals, and you can achieve more than imagined. There are enough successes and dollars to go around. Affirm that money comes easily to you and that you are resourceful. There is never a need to worry about money when your energy, mindset, and actions align with increasing value and inviting financial success.

Create a list of financial affirmations and intentions to replace beliefs that focus on money instead of value. Affirmations such as:

- I am financially free.
- I am worthy of financial success.
- I am on a path to build wealth.
- My income exceeds my expenses.
- I can make my financial dreams my reality.

Intentions such as:

- I intend to save with purpose.
- I intend to spend in alignment with my values and goals.
- I intend to surround myself with financially like-minded people.
- I intend to increase my net worth.
- I intend to prioritize my financial goals.

Journal your affirmations and intentions to replace limiting beliefs. Review and recite daily.

2. Express gratitude and live gratefully.

To raise vibrational energy and self-awareness, consider all that you already have. If you're grateful, then anything more you receive is extra. Take inventory of your life and express gratitude for everything you have. You'll notice that over time, your focus shifts from what you *do not* have to what you have. Thinking in terms of abundance mutes and eliminates a scarcity mindset.

Have you noticed that people who complain about money are always complaining about money? A mindset based on limitations is a mindset of neediness. You have the power to create an abundant reality. Evolve your mind to invite what you want into your life. Be grateful, as if you have already received the financial stability and wealth you desire. Gratitude for the financial abundance we have makes financial goals feel less of a challenge. Focusing on the present is at the root of a success mindset.

3. Visualize financial success.

Once we feel and believe money is abundant, worry, stress, and concern about money subside. See yourself financially successful and having more than enough to meet your financial goals. A vision board can be helpful here. Add to your vision board (or create a new one solely for this purpose) with specific images related to you and your financial goals. Be sure not to clutter the board and to be clear with your choice of images.

If you can't see yourself financially successful, repeat step 1. Your spending and saving habits should be in alignment with your values and goals. Without alignment, your actions may be more harmful than good. Explore feelings that accompany achieving financial success as you visualize.

4. Practice having money.

When you have opportunities to save money, save it! If you're always spending money, then you're always going to want money and never have it. Saving enhances your relationship with money. Start simple. Eat out and purchase alcohol less. Use coupons and shop on discount days. Refrain from impulse purchases and instant gratification. Review your financial statements, track spending, and understand your cash flow needs each month. As you save and your financial wealth increases, you'll notice less of a need to spend money unnecessarily, and your financial decisions will improve.

The more mindful you are of your financial goals, competing with others and purchasing things only because you can, are no longer appealing to you. Consult guidance from a knowledgeable financial advisor, family member, or trusted friend to help tailor spending habits and develop a financial plan that places you on the offensive instead of the defensive in your relationship with money. As your financial decisions and actions improve, you'll invite more money into your life by investing in yourself, your dreams, and your ambitions. When the lack of money is no longer a concern, financial survival and material things no longer define you. Become empowered and feel inspired to help others in economic despair find their financial footing and path. Contributing to the lives of others invites abundance. Contribute value, and you will receive tenfold!

Having money and being financially successful comes down to who you are, what you want, and the changes you make to invite everything that is for you. We could blame our unfavorable financial disposition on our childhood, others' actions, lack of opportunities and information, the economy and market, but how far does blaming anyone or anything get us? Nowhere. Transformation comes by being uncomfortable and living in the present. What can you do today to position yourself for financial success? What daily habits will allow you to have continued progress? Financial success does not happen overnight, so take baby steps in developing sustainable practices. Successful baby steps leap us forward toward improvement.

Many of us assume we know everything there is to know and that we're doing the best we can, but are we? Challenge yourself to seek your truth and be comfortable with being uncomfortable. By peeling back the layers of ego, we can discover our underlying motivation to be financially successful. Understand your why. Motivation and confidence land differently when they're driven by your knowledge, passions, and values. Do you have what it takes to be financially successful? Until we take full responsibility for ourselves and everything that happens to us, achieving financial success is just fog on a summer morning. You may be able to see it, but you can never touch it. Believe in yourself and enhance your relationship with money to invite abundance into your life.

TIME FOR REFLECTION

My perceived measure of success is:

When I think of my financial success, I see it as:

A limiting belief I've had about financial success is:

Financially, I am grateful that I have:

I intend to express gratitude by:

I intend to add the following financial goals to my vision board:

From now on, I intend to save $____________ amount every ____________.

I intend to seek financial guidance from:

CHAPTER FOURTEEN

The Voice from the Ceiling

"Be brave enough to live the life of your dreams according to your vision and purpose instead of the expectations and opinions of others."
—Roy T. Bennett

FOR MANY YEARS while living in New York, I attended church on Sundays with Grandma Pearl. She was always excited to have my brothers and me at her side as she greeted her church family. Sunday school was before the main church service, so my brothers and I knew it would be a long day on any given Sunday spent with grandma. As a kid, I was restless in church. I would wiggle in my seat, stare at the ceiling, make annoying noises, and daydream my way through the sermon.

On this one Sunday, the pastor reflected on becoming the anointed leader of the church. The pastor explained God told him to be a pastor. As children, we take everything literally. I envisioned a deep voice coming from the ceiling, saying, "You should be a pastor." The pastor said he knew he was on a path destined for him because of the joy and blessings he had received. I recall looking at the ceiling and listening for a "voice" to tell me what to do. (Never heard the voice.) The pastor referenced an inner voice guiding him to align his actions with his passions, values, and spiritual connection. As I reflected on the sermon over the years, the sermon was not about God speaking vocally to the pastor. The sermon was about the pastor uncovering and living out his purpose.

Many of us spend a lifetime in search of purpose and fulfillment. Some of us find purpose quicker than others. Others never discover purpose at all. Purpose is the underlying motive for action, the reason we get up in the morning, and the relentless, passionate drive to be our best selves.

Before I found purpose, there was a nagging uneasiness that created a hunger for belongingness and excitement. Daily routines and experiences felt mundane and scripted. Thoughts and actions did not seem reflective of my authentic self. I woke up every morning taking inventory of my life and feeling like my successes, no matter how great, were not enough. Motivation to succeed without purpose is not sustainable and leads to conditional happiness. Once I became aware of my passions and aligned with my values, life became more fruitful than ever.

From a young age, I've heard, "You have a way with words." The gravity of that statement fell blindly on me, and I never saw its value until about fifteen years ago as I matured in the investments industry. As my investment knowledge and confidence grew, my speaking ability and presentation skills shined more than ever. Years later, I received a promotion with the responsibility of traveling the US and inspiring financial professionals to achieve better investment outcomes for their clients at conferences and workshops. Public speaking and inspiring audiences felt natural and exhilarating! My message delivery and authentic connection with audiences gave financial professionals the will to commit to positive change and increase their success by using the firm's advice. The new role did not feel like work, but part of a much greater plan. The blueprint God provides is always grander than the diagram we offer ourselves. I woke up every day excited for the opportunity to make a difference and passionately give more value. The more value I gave, the happier and more at peace I became.

Passionately and selflessly giving ourselves through our beliefs and values to receive abundance is what the pastor was communicating to the congregation.

Beyond my career, my studies and practices as a student of life deepened. I don't know if any of us become a master of life, but I have embraced a personal mission to try. I began a journey of redefining my values and minimizing limiting beliefs. Every morning started with an expression of gratitude and reciting "I am" affirmations to kick off the day. I found myself vibrantly uplifted and thinking about opportunities for selfless sacrifice. The "how" was not as important as the "why," which enabled me to trust the process. By setting the intentions and affirming my life success goals, my thoughts and actions followed suit and invited abundance into my life. I saw each day as an opportunity to be a better person and be more for more people.

I watched self-help videos and read personal growth books on topics such as public speaking, leadership, purpose, rapport, wealth, and many more. I wanted to serve and inspire others in the most significant way. My knowledge and confidence grew. I found myself fascinated with the mind and developed an optimistic outlook that positively affected my feelings, thoughts, and outcomes. I became my excitement and uncovered my purpose: to inspire successful outcomes in the lives of others. Purpose was right under my nose the entire time!

As my mindset evolved, I had conversations with friends, family, associates, and strangers, where we shared personal experiences, growth stories, and different perspectives. My perceived reality broadened, and I viewed myself and my communities differently. Self-respect increased, boundaries formed, and the people in my life changed. Friends and family viewed me as an example. I became a sounding board, an advocate, and a source of inspiration in the good and bad times. Countless opportunities emerged to contribute value to the lives of others. Every encounter became purposeful and played a role in my thoughts and actions. I wanted to do more and help others with whatever they desired! To be successful at anything, it takes knowledge, practice, and execution. So I mastered life coaching concepts and became a certified professional life coach.

I evoked awareness and provided a voice of support, accountability, and encouragement to those who wanted a guide on their journey. People began to self-discover, see, feel, and believe that they can achieve whatever they want. We have to give value to receive value. As clients found the will to commit to their journey and pursue their life desires, I lived a life of joy and fulfillment as the pastor preached about on that one Sunday. Figuratively, the deep voice from the ceiling told me to, "Inspire and help others evolve their mindset and actions to achieve happiness and success." Selfless sacrifice has presented itself, and I can provide solutions my way.

At last, I am living a healed and purpose-driven life.

A lot of us live our lives based on limiting beliefs or someone's expectations. Do you know your purpose? Do you know who you are? What are your passions? We uncover our passions and purpose as we connect with who we are, change our mindset, and form an impactful vision.

What is the importance of living with purpose? Finding your purpose elevates vibrational energy and places you on the path to achieving long-term fulfillment. Life moves fast, and before we know it, we look up and have taken on a lot of endeavors that now define us. We become lost and confused about what happiness looks like for us. Living with purpose and being aligned with our passions and values focuses on our feelings, decisions, and inviting abundance. Purpose brings meaning to everything we do and is unique to us. Our experiences, passions, and abilities to contribute value vary, but we all have a purpose.

Many of us have the aching feeling that we should be doing more or something different to enjoy life. Julia Cameron, an American teacher, said, "What we want to do is what we are meant to do. When we do what we are meant to do, money comes to us, doors open for us, we feel useful, and the work we do feels like play to us."

Do you ever wake up and feel as if you're going through the motions? What about snoozing the morning away because you dread the day ahead? Ask yourself, what would it take for you to be excited? Do you live for weekends, holidays, and summers? Once you find your purpose, life becomes enjoyable, and you want to be your best at all times. You feel vibrant, and the invisible wall blocking happiness, peace, and success dissolves. You're able to craft thoughts and pursue your short-term goals with patient action. Your vision for successful outcomes is happening now! You find yourself sharing ideas and inspiration. Excitement and energy exude as you become aware of your purpose and shift your mindset.

Searching for our purpose can be a daunting and draining activity if we don't know where to begin or feel confused about who we are. We feel as if our purpose should jump out right in front of us. The discovery of our purpose can be the single most defining moment of our existence! Find your truth. The larger the expected outcome of our desires, the more energy, awareness, thoughts, and actions are necessary to invite what we want into our lives.

So, where do we start?

To uncover our purpose, we must rediscover who we are and reveal our passions. Many of us frame thoughts about purpose by starting from the point of success, such as businesses that provide value and make money. We force success based on outcomes that misalign with our values and passions. It's easy to see someone fulfilled and living out their dreams and say, "I can do that." You may find success doing the same or a similar endeavor, but success for you will be limited if your energy, values, and passions are not in alignment with the same goal to the same degree.

DISCOVERING YOUR PURPOSE

Before you review these steps, take time to meditate, get out your journal, and even go to your playground.

1. Who are you?

Understanding who you are and acknowledging your strengths is the best place to start. Review your values and make a list of traits that sum you up as parts of a whole. Do you like running the show or being a part of the show? Are you outgoing or reserved? Are you creative or analytical? Do you see the glass half-full or half-empty? What are the qualities that make you feel impactful to your family and communities? For example, I'm a risk-taker and an expressive communicator. Evaluate yourself based on your authentic self, not the expectations or thoughts of others. Discovery of yourself is your chance to be great.

2. What are your passions?

Everything begins with vibrational energy! Passion transforms us into a ball of vibrant energy and drives us to make the impossible *possible*. Our passions fuel the value we can provide the world through our purpose. I'm a passionate learner of life and people. When we think and talk about our desires, everything feels perfect, and we smile with our mouths and eyes.

Consider and list your passions. If you're passionate about creating and expressing art, write down art. A passion, no matter how small, has the potential to make an impact greater than imagined. Steve Jobs said, "People with passion can change the world." Write your passions regardless of limiting notions. Your passions eagerly motivate and inspire you to master a concept, activity, or cause. Perhaps home robots, personal fitness, or basket-weaving interest you! Passion comes from within and gracefully drives our emotions, thoughts, and actions.

3. What are you good at that you enjoy?

There's an activity or something you do exceptionally well that makes people notice. What is it? The activity could be fixing laptops, singing cover songs, recommending travel destinations, or writing short stories. I'm good at connecting with and serving people. Consider activities and causes that you enjoy and make you feel great as you do them. What are they? As you complete this step, stretch beyond the limiting beliefs by considering activities you enjoy and may find challenging but are intriguing to you. For example, I enjoy and am intrigued by public speaking but find it challenging.

The difference between a passion and an activity you're good at is that you can be passionate about something but not necessarily good at it. You can be good at something but not necessarily passionate about it too. For example, you may enjoy fixing ceiling fans, but you're not passionate about it. One could be passionate about baseball and enjoy coaching baseball but not currently good at coaching. Write the activities you find pleasurable and do well. Also, write the activities you enjoy that require work to become proficient or exceptional. The combination of exercises will help you narrow down your focus later. If you're passionate about an activity or cause, you'll discover the right path and training to become masterful. Wherever we focus our energy and time, momentum and practice will drive mastery.

4. How can you serve others by doing what you love *and* make money?

This step is where the rubber meets the road. We were born with unique talents and gifts to contribute to the world. Why do people seem to praise or thank you? Is it your wittiness or comedic nature? Maybe your purpose is to be a comedian and brighten the days of others with laughter. Or perhaps cooking is your thing, and you enjoy serving those without the time or energy to cook for themselves. Maybe you find pleasure in influencing teenagers that need one-on-one guidance.

Before considering money, think in terms of selfless sacrifice—the contribution of value without self. When I was a local run club member, I offered tips to improve running form, speed, and breathing. Over time, the run club members looked to me for running guidance. I then became a run coach for the run club by accepting an offer which paid me for my coaching abilities. Giving the best of ourselves selflessly today can lead to monetary rewards tomorrow. If you can serve or provide without receiving money, who would you help? Who do you think benefits the most when serving selflessly? Believe it or not, you do!

Perhaps you would enjoy consulting for small businesses to improve sales. Focus on the highest value you can provide serving others. The money will follow—the more significant the impact you have on your communities, the more excellent the monetary reward. Consider your value proposition to define your targeted clientele; the value you provide to invite people to pay for your offerings. As a run coach, I was passionate about speed training, so I offered specialized speed-training schedules tailored to specific abilities and goals. List as many ideas as you can. Who you are, your values and your passions should drive your thoughts and help define the people you would like to serve.

At the end of the exercise, you have several ideas to consider. The exercise should be an intentional journey of self-exploration instead of a homework assignment. Have fun finding you! You now have lists of your passions and activities, so let's narrow the possibilities. Review the lists and group your passions and activities by common themes. For example, if your passions and activities have health and fitness in common, group them.

As you complete this step, you may notice a few outliers that do not have a home or common theme. Group the outliers and ask yourself, what excites me about each one? You may find that many of the outliers do not excite you as much as you thought. If you can't think of a reason an outlier excites you, cross it out. For instance, you may have listed home training dogs. As you ponder the patience required and note that patience is not one of your values, eliminate home training dogs from your list. Although training dogs may not be your purpose, you can still have an interest and allocate your time to the cause differently.

Repeat the thought process for the remaining outliers. Keep the outliers that continue to excite you on the list. Repeat this process for your grouped passions and activities. As you reduce the number of passions and activities that you enjoy to a few, look for combinations between the passions and activities that excite you. Perhaps you have a passion for guitars (passion list), and you're good at and enjoy teaching (activity list). Maybe teaching guitar could be your purpose. Write the combination down if it excites you. Make your way through the lists, focusing only on what excites you and eliminating those that don't excite you.

As you narrow and frame your thoughts, bounce ideas off trusted people in your life. Many times, we can limit ourselves based on the borders of our imaginations. Others may help us think outside the box or be more innovative with our findings. Since your ideas align with who you are, your passions, what you enjoy, and who you want to serve, there is no harm in getting thoughts from an objective perspective. Fully explore inspirational ideas that you can see yourself doing for the rest of your life. Do not become anxious, focused on money, or think that you need to figure out your purpose overnight. Forcing anything does not align with positive outcomes. We can only observe the beauty of the forest once we relax and step back from the trees. Your mind is fertile, and you have planted the seeds of possibilities. By going through the exercise, you can create a mindful environment that promotes visualization and awareness.

If you need opportunities to discover your passions or what you enjoy, then volunteer! Volunteering is a great way to apply your gifts and serve others selflessly while gaining insight and new experiences. Maybe volunteering at an animal rescue would excite you more than home training dogs. I volunteered for a nonprofit and discovered a passion for education. We don't know what we don't know.

Find out more about yourself by discovering and rediscovering your passions by broadening your experiences. Take lessons, attend classes, and speak with subject matter experts in the field or endeavor where you have an interest. I have a friend who tries out a new activity or endeavor every year for the entire year. If you would like to learn more about a particular business, grab coffee or lunch with someone who's already making it happen. Their knowledge can become your knowledge, allowing you to generate ideas and learn more about your passions. Idea sharing is how the most extraordinary things in life became great. Think big, apply your passions, and fuel your interests with information. As your knowledge increases about you and your passions, vibrational energy elevates, and you gain clarity on your purpose.

Nothing worthwhile happens without action. Generating ideas and developing a vision is great, but talking is one thing, and doing is another. Focus on a central idea that gets you feeling good and then redirect your energy, emotions, and thoughts to design the first step to materialize your vision. Consider short-term goals to incite momentum and progress. Setting two to three short-term goals every other week while setting more or loftier goals once a month may work as well. You decide on the number of goals and frequency that works for you—quality over quantity.

This book did not just happen. The project began with donating my knowledge, thoughts, and guidance to my communities. As I communicated with passion, an idea formed to inspire and guide others by sharing my life experiences and knowledge on paper. I saw myself as an author and a guide to inspire happiness and success. From there, I formed goals that led to chapters and, ultimately, a book. The setting of achievable short-term goals made the passionate idea a reality. As you visualize yourself thriving at your happiest and successfully carrying out your purpose, the vision for each step leads to patient but deliberate actions. Nothing great comes from being reactionary or unintentional. Intentionally let what comes, come and what goes, go. We can live out our dreams once we let go of doubt and fears.

You'll know you're on the right path as the next step reveals itself with minimal resistance. Each step will not be easy since challenges and obstacles are intentionally inviting growth opportunities and preparing you for success. Let go of the outcome and enjoy the journey!

TIME FOR REFLECTION

My traits are:

My passions/hobbies are:

I'm good at and enjoy:

I absolutely love: ______________________________________ but need more education on the topic.

If I could serve or provide for anyone without receiving money in return, I would:

The common theme here is:

CHAPTER FIFTEEN

Success Is in the Purpose of the Journey

"Our goals can only be reached through a vehicle of a plan, in which we must fervently believe, and upon which we must vigorously act. There is no other route to success."
—Pablo Picasso

I'VE ALWAYS HAD a strong affection for the financial markets and growing wealth. I have enjoyed watching movies such as *Trading Places, Wall Street, Boiler Room,* and *The Wolf of Wall Street* and felt envious of the lofty lifestyles and adrenaline rush of chasing the big score. Of course, the money in the movies goes as fast as it comes, but the suspense and possibilities that come along with taking massive risks were exhilarating! As a lifetime member of the finance discipline, I assure you measured risk is the best way to go. Leave the "rags-to-riches, riches-to-rags" stories for the movies.

The compounding effect associated with growing financial assets spearheaded my curiosity about investments. Increasing $1 to $2 with proper planning and spending habits leads to financial success! Pretty impressive if you think about it.

My financial services career began as a check processing clerk followed by a 1-800 call center associate during the last years of college.

The jobs were nothing sensational, but anything can provide value if we have a success mindset. I was a self-funded college student with big dreams and visualized a life after college beyond living comfortably. My master plan had to go into effect immediately to materialize the vision. I was a poor college student, but my mindset was that of a successful CEO.

There are no delays for progress other than procrastination and perfection. When others were partying, I was visualizing. When others were drinking, I was networking. When others were sleeping, I was dreaming. I have always been an optimist and like to challenge the mind to believe and see more than meets the eye. To fly to the greatest heights, I mapped out an optimal but flexible flight path and designed a plane that could soar without limits: *me*. Finding my way into the field of investments after college and working with the financial markets were the primary objectives and key to my adult life unfolding as intended. Every larger goal had smaller goals or near-term checkpoints to drive momentum and minimize stalling. Short-term goals were mini trampolines to launch me toward the next level of success.

To begin the flight towards a thriving career, I reviewed job descriptions for senior-level leadership positions within the investment industry that aligned with my passions and values. This exercise was not to tease me with unreachable qualifications or earnings but to understand the strengths demanded by the marketplace. Setting the intention to strengthen my skillsets encouraged me to focus only on what I can control: my actions today to set up a bright future for tomorrow.

I knew specific skills were transferable to other industries, so my efforts and time would not go to waste. Skill strengthening became the focus. I created short, intermediate, and long-term goals to become an articulate communicator, enhance interpersonal skills, and sharpen attention to detail.

After defining these goals, writing them down, and setting intentions, I practiced developing my skills by being more present and vocal in group conversations, team meetings, and classroom settings. I connected with individuals on a deeper level and became better a worker, classmate, friend, and family member. People noticed. The *right* people noticed. I developed a one-of-a-kind presence in just about everything I did.

One day as I began my shift, a senior leader at the call center pulled me aside and said, "You're different. Keep your nose clean, know your stuff, and good things will happen for you." I stared at him like a deer in headlights, in confusion by his reference and compliment.

I puzzlingly said, "Thank you."

The leader then asked that I walk with him back to his desk. Once we arrived, he handed me a best-selling guide on résumé writing from his bookshelf for me to keep. The leader also gave me the name and phone number of a local headhunter to speak with for career guidance. This gesture was like receiving twenty bars of gold and the keys to the city—we know the value, but the gift is only meaningful if we do something with it. I was grateful for his time, advice, and gift. The encounter seemed unreal since we had never crossed paths before, nor did we ever have a conversation—not even about the weather.

Encounters such as the one with the senior leader have happened throughout my life. Guides emerge to confirm our path, assist, or redirect us along the way. All we have to do is pay attention. Anyone successful will be the first to tell you they did not become successful on their own. Who has given you the keys to the city? Did you recognize it at the time? How did you make use of the gift?

The day after graduation, I accepted a position in the company's wealth and asset management division. By centering my thoughts on short-term goals and embracing what I had, opportunities appeared, and positive encounters helped me enter the industry I desired. By setting intentional goals, being mindful, and taking deliberate action, I embarked on the flight path that led me to the heights of success that I experience today.

We commit to goals with a motivating desire to experience a specific outcome. Whether the goal is simple, like setting the alarm to wake or launching a profitable practice, goals are essential to navigating through life. Without goals, we find ourselves going through the motions, limiting our success, and creating unintentional realities.

There is a correlation between the importance of the goal to the individual and the magnitude of the result. The more important the goal is to the person pursuing the goal, the more committed the individual will be to achieve the goal and the more outstanding the outcome. If the goal does not have meaning or importance, the action plan becomes negotiable and less likely to be completed. Our will to succeed has to be unwavering and driven by emotion. Challenging goals require effort and commitment to realize success. Attempting to accomplish any goal for the approval, acceptance, or validation of others provides little success since robust energy and resilient emotion are necessary to align the mind, thoughts, and actions. We have to own the goal for ourselves to achieve fulfillment. If we cannot feel, believe, or see the achievement of our goals, we create resistance. We can set the alarm to wake up at a particular time, but we must set the intention to get up at that time. Otherwise, we will snooze away our goal.

Goals must align with our values to be meaningful and generate the energy, emotion, and action required. Do your goals align with your values? Sustainable happiness is in the progress towards the goal, not the achievement of the goal. Have you ever pursued a goal, and once achieved, the pleasure from the outcome wore off? The highest point of gratification fades at the precise moment we reach the goal. The successful outcome is the icing on the cake that we baked by setting the goal and executing actions.

Listen to a grandparent talk about past success. Ninety-nine percent of the story is going to pertain to the journey, not the result. As we become wiser from observations and experiences, we conclude goals do not equal happiness. Happiness arrives when we are connected with the journey to achieve the goal, detached from the outcome. Joy should be present throughout the journey as progress occurs and not delayed until the end.

Suppose we don't achieve the goal as expected or in the time estimated. Are we not happy with the progress and feedback? We have zero control over the goal itself, but we control how we feel and think as we progress toward the goal.

Happiness is in the progress. The more significant the progress on the journey, the greater the level of satisfaction experienced. Progress toward goals gives us a direction, generates positive emotions, and encourages us to keep going. Set milestones and checkpoints along the way to reduce doubts and affirm our intentions for continued progress. The accomplishment of our goals gives us additional satisfaction with the progress that supports our happiness.

We achieve goals with action. We can think, dream, and manifest all we want, but progress toward our goals cannot happen until there is action. Positive energy and emotions attribute to positive actions. Positive actions deliver positive results. This book could not exist without committing myself to intentional motivations and putting pen to paper. The book you're reading today would not exist without action. As I write this book, my only focus is to ensure that each sentence is meaningful and expresses thought as intended. In other words, mini-goals! The goal of writing a book is the outcome of a gazillion mini-goals. As I complete each mini-goal, my gratitude and sense of fulfillment increases as each page writes itself with conscious thought.

Happiness emerged through the journey of writing this book. The finished book is the icing on the cake. If we understand the source of our joy and live as if we have achieved our goals, we can direct greater emotion toward each step and create value. It's the blend of emotions, thoughts, and actions that lead to progress and the most desirable outcomes. Develop a successful and repeatable method to achieve your goals.

ACHIEVING YOUR GOALS

The emotions and thoughts that accompany the goal-setting process motivate, inspire, and give us the confidence to execute actions that align with the expected outcome. The value in goal-setting is in the process. Goal-setting centers your energy toward the desired outcome and can influence intentional thoughts and actions to make your goal a reality. If we don't set meaningful goals, the emotion that drives successful thoughts and actions will not be there.

1. Define a goal that inspires you.

We set goals with intention and passion to achieve successful outcomes. If your goal is to become an expert in your field within the next three years and you have recently entered the industry, victory may be doubtful without having intentional short-term goals and the passionate drive to learn and apply as much as possible. Anything is possible when we are passionate. Defining, pursuing, and achieving goals begins within you. Connect and align your goals with your values to ensure that the goal is *for* you. The goal gains strength and weight in our perceived realities when we mindfully consider the purpose and how the goal relates to us. Anything that has strength and value to us affects our emotions, mindset, and actions.

Start by setting visionary goals, such as where you would like to be in the next five years. Move onto smaller goals that align with your visionary goal and pursue them in the near-to-intermediate term. Define goals that motivate you and invite the outcomes you envision.

Many of us miss the mark with goal-setting because we are not specific or set too many goals at once. As you may have seen before, your goals should be SMART (specific, measurable, attainable, realistic, and timely). Setting SMART goals is a great way to ensure we are setting goals that intentionally position us for success.

With practice, you can discover goal-setting and execution methods that work for you. There are multiple ways to achieve goals, but most methods have similar concepts, such as:

1. Know and set the goal with a date in mind.
2. Commit to the goal.
3. Visualize and see yourself achieving the goal.
4. Plan and take intentional actions.
5. Be accountable in pursuit of the goal.

Begin your goal-setting process by defining where in your life you would like to make intentional progress. What is the goal? Write it down. Does the goal align with your values? Why is the goal important to you? Write it down. Do you believe you can achieve the goal? What are you willing to do to replace limiting beliefs? For example, I did not think that I performed well on camera. To replace the limiting belief, I watched over fifty videos of various speakers to sharpen my on-camera skills. Do I look directly at the camera? What if I mess up? How do I look natural? The more videos I watched, and the more I visualized myself in front of the camera, the more I believed I could be a star on camera. Mindset changes actions and actions change everything. Can you see yourself achieving the goal?

You must be able to see yourself achieving the goal and believe that you can achieve the goal with no doubt. Don't be a doubter. Doubters are overthinkers who limit themselves to wishing. You are not a wisher. You are a passionate believer who intentionally achieves. Know the difference.

2. Develop a plan with flexibility.

Some of us have impressive goals but don't have excellent plans to achieve them. We either didn't have a plan at all or didn't have an adequate plan with flexibility. Rigid plans don't work because life is fluid. Developing a plan with a date materializes the goal. Nothing positive happens without a date, so set a realistic one. For example, you are planning to be an expert in three years. To select a date for your goal, you want to learn as much as possible about the experts in your field today, such as how did they become so knowledgeable? What makes them an expert? What was their flight path? What can you learn from them? Determine and absorb the necessary information to increase the probability of a successful outcome.

After defining the goal and estimating a date, let's focus on achieving the goal. Outline the first step. Write it down. After the first step, think about the next step and so on. Outline the steps, set milestones, and checkpoints with flexible time frames and dates. If you need additional information, the first step may be to research the steps and actions. The objective here is to progress toward the goal. With the expert example, you may start by narrowing your scope, gathering supporting materials, and researching training programs. As you receive the information you need, motivation grows, and the possibilities become more apparent. Suppose there are question marks for the later stages of your goal-achieving journey, no big deal. Don't sweat it. We don't have to uncover every step during the first goal-setting session. Revisit the goal over multiple sessions and tweak the steps as you make progress. Establish periodic goal sessions, daily or weekly, not to focus on the goal itself but to focus on the current and next steps.

Once you're on track and executing each step to the best of your ability, the next step becomes clearer, doubt dissipates, and knowledge grows. If you don't know where to begin, connect with people and resources that can provide insight into the process to achieve your specific goal. Do your homework. Not everyone gives unbiased advice, so set your standards for success. The more you embed yourself in the realm of what you want to achieve, the more natural and tangible the goal becomes.

3. Track progress toward the goal.

Without metrics, we are rolling the dice and hoping for the best. Do better and be better. Hold yourself accountable by monitoring progress. Are you completing each step by the estimated date? If not, maybe your dates are too aggressive. Have you ever pursued a goal and were too adamant about the date of the outcome? The journey probably became burdensome, frustrating, and stressful.

Operating at low vibrational frequencies invigorates doubt and blocks the flow of progress and momentum. A vision board can help maintain positive vibes toward the goal. Perhaps having images of the business you would like to start or company you want to work with as an industry expert could help. Set yourself up to succeed by completing the steps in a reasonable amount of time. Adjust time frames and dates based on the complexity of each step or task. Flexibility enables you to reignite motivation, change course, and continue progress toward the goal.

If you struggle to getting through materials or networking to broaden your knowledge, figure out what you need to do to achieve your goal, adjust, and make it happen. We, as go-getters, can get in our way. Detach yourself from the goal to create space for progress and happiness. Remember, you have no control over the outcome, but you do have control over each step and task along the way. Focus on delivering the highest value and quality with your efforts.

With proper execution, the outcome you desire becomes within reach and arrives as you intended. Let the goal come to you based on your emotions, mindset, and actions. Complete each step with intention.

Having an accountability partner can help improve your goal-seeking journey. Studies show that those who set tasks for their goals and track progress every week, with encouraging peers, are 40 percent more likely to achieve their goals.[11] Partner with someone who is soundly familiar with the goal or working on a similar goal. For becoming an industry expert, your accountability partner may be someone who is already an expert or further along than you are. Your accountability partner is there to help you be accountable to yourself. Meeting with your partner and discussing steps, accomplishments, milestones, and checkpoints can continually fuel your drive to succeed. The sharing of experiences and exchanging of thoughts and ideas improve the journey and results. You do not have to go it alone, my friend.

Success happens when motivation and action deliver results. If your efforts are not working, revisit step 1. Could your motivation be stagnant or lacking? Are you forcing tasks or steps that are not in alignment? Revisiting "you" helps determine if the goal needs to be adjusted or if there are better actions that can invite success. The fastest way to a goal is not always the best way to achieve the goal. The most complex route to achieve a goal does not always lead to the best outcome, either. Check-in with yourself often and reevaluate each step as your knowledge, motivation, and confidence increase. There are limitless ways to accomplish each step, but it's up to you to discover the most optimal way to close the gap between where you are and the successful outcome you desire.

As you complete each step and achieve the goal, celebrate your accomplishments no matter how big or small! Celebrate every victory.

11 Kath Kyle, "10 Goal Setting Statistics: Research Studies Facts & Findings," Blog, accessed March 12, 2021, https://www.kathkyle.com/goal-setting-statistics/.

Plan mini-rewards that continue to motivate and inspire you with each milestone. Positive reinforcement is essential, mentally and emotionally, to your wellness. Moving to the next step or goal without embellishing in the glory of achievement marginalizes the success of the journey and fulfillment. Bask in the glory of each accomplishment and reflect on the journey. You did it!

The goal-defining process begins by focusing on you. The actual achievement of the goal ends with you, not the goal. Are there lessons learned you can carry over to other goals? Write them down. Have you become a better person? How so? Achieving goals is about you. The faster you realize this concept, the less challenging pursuing and achieving your goals will be.

TIME FOR REFLECTION

My visionary goal is:

My mini-goals to achieve my visionary goal are:

This goal is important to me because:

To achieve this goal, I intend to replace the following limiting beliefs:

I intend to add the following milestones and checkpoints with times and dates to my vision board:

I intend to track the progress toward my goal by:

I celebrate victories by:

CHAPTER SIXTEEN

Make the Mission Possible

"Some people want it to happen, some wish it would happen, others make it happen."
—Michael Jordan

GROWING UP IN New York from age six through adolescence, basketball became my sport of choice. On any day, I was on a blacktop court at a local school or public playground playing a twenty-one or half-court three-on-three game. I played pickup games with people from all walks of life, old and young, and learned the game from my cousin and undiscovered superstars. The popular basketball courts were in crime-ridden neighborhoods. Many of us were there to play a clean and fun game of basketball, while others were there to disrupt or create an atmosphere of hostility. It didn't take long to learn how to navigate between the troublesome inner-city meccas across town and rose-colored suburban streets where I lived. Having a clique from the inner city gave me ease, knowing that I had backup if a tussle emerged.

These bonds became negative influences. I developed two personas. I made student of the month but entertained a scuffle during study hall. I helped Mom with Saturday errands but defied authority figures. Praises were limited and often came with some element of disappointment. My behavior was bewildering to my parents and teachers since I was a "good kid" and had access to communities and resources that supported success.

We often don't see the opportunities when we focus on the wrong things. After getting in trouble for joyriding in a neighbor's car, a change was necessary. I empowered myself by taking responsibility for my reality with heavy encouragement from Dad, of course. At that moment, at age thirteen, I became focused on transitioning my life in a better direction.

A growth journey began by being curious and holding myself accountable for the transformation I envisioned for myself. It isn't enough for others to want change *for* us. We have to want the change for ourselves more than anyone for change to happen and be sustainable.

I started playing basketball in membership gyms, organized venues, and college campuses instead of rough neighborhoods. I joined intramural basketball organizations and played on the school team. The more I changed my environment and sought out influences that aligned with and supported my desires to succeed, the more my thoughts, actions, and outcomes changed. I adopted the West Point Military Academy's Honor Code: "A cadet will not lie, cheat, steal, or tolerate those who do." I became a positive influence on others—forming productive relationships.

I started reading beyond school assignments with a focus on biographies, history, and adventure. As my interests evolved, my perspective broadened, and my behavior mirrored excellence. My positive intentions materialized, and the importance of self-education became crystal clear. I took up track and field and cross-country running, which strengthened my mind and showed me the value of discipline. Sports can provide us with an understanding that the mind controls the body and pain is temporary—lessons that can carryover to other areas of life.

Today, I connect the success in my life to replacing limiting beliefs and changing my mindset over thirty years ago. Everything back then and thereafter have become the fabric for who I am.

We can become whoever we want to become. The limitations of our perceived realities can sweep us away, or we can replace them and grow to live extraordinary lives. Change is unavoidable, and growth is optional. Choose growth over the status quo.

What was your moment that sparked change? Perhaps your moment is right now. How will your growth journey begin? Nothing can happen without making it happen. Actions that align with our values and a success mindset invite positive growth. Living in the moment, having the right attitude, and taking advantage of the avenues and opportunities presented is the secret to success. If we rely only on praying, wanting, wishing, and hoping without intentional action, we experience more praying, wanting, wishing, and hoping. Action is necessary to make a new reality possible.

We have everything within us to have and do whatever we want at any point in our lives. Some of us find comfort in complaining about our perceived reality or are fearful of change. Others of us have underlying emotional and mental blockers and disruptors that prevent us from being great. When we let complaining and being fearful define us, our perceived realities reflect our limitations. Develop habits that align with your values and desires, and success can happen for you.

How can we expect people to treat us with respect if we don't respect ourselves? How can we expect others to love us if we don't love ourselves? If we don't believe we can be successful, can we be successful?

Many of us subconsciously surround ourselves with those who complain and are fearful of uncertainty and success. Misery loves company, right? We can quickly become complacent and settle for living a life that is less than envisioned. The people we surround ourselves with, the food we eat, where we live, our fitness choices, and the books and entertainment we engage with reflect who we are. Do you like what you see? What is stopping you from being the best version of yourself? What prevents you from achieving the level of success you desire? Probably 99.99 percent of the time, the answer to the last question is Y-O-U. You are in the way of your greatness. Success does not magically arrive on your doorstep. Make the mission possible with intentional action.

Are you happy with the life you are living? Are you pleased with the choices you are making? Make today the day that you change your mindset, take action, and place yourself on a path of limitless success. Once you define success for yourself and see yourself being successful, the proper habits and actions will lead you to all you deserve.

TAKING ACTION

Every day, we have a choice to move forward or standstill. We can have goals that sound good, but dreams do not become our reality until we apply intentional actions. You have the power to transform your life. Steps are below that can guide you in creating progress after goal-setting.

1. Change your focus.

Where we place our focus is what expands. The mind can create, prevent, and destroy successful outcomes. Be deliberate and intentional about focusing your energy, thoughts, and actions to achieve desired results. Focusing on pain or the past does not move you toward healing and growth, nor does it encourage actions. Worrying hampers the mind and leads you to take actions that cause more harm than good. When you focus on emotional mastery and practice mindfulness, you're in control of you and can take actions that align with your desired outcome. Anyone can start a plan, but not everyone can complete a task as intended. Let go of the end to focus on each step of the journey.

When I trained to become a certified professional coach, my emotions and thoughts focused on mastering the topics at hand. My focus was not on the achievement of the certification. The certification was just a reflection of my mastery of the subjects taught during the coaching program. Center your attention on taking the action that brings you value as if you've already succeeded. The burning desire of want or lack will not fog near-term decision-making or actions.

Focusing on high-value actions begins with deciding what goal you want to achieve. Once you decide on the goal, write it down with a date to embed the goal into the subconscious mind. Most people will continue to dwell on the goal until the goal becomes a self-fulfilling prophecy, and then disappointment ensues. We're not doing that. Instead, you will shift your focus to thoughts and actions that bring you closer to the goal. Ask yourself a series of questions, such as, what can I do now to prepare me to pursue my goal? How can I prioritize focus toward achieving my goal? What support do I need to be successful? Prompting your mind to dig deeper into your connection with the goal draws energy and focus toward defining the proper path to intentional success.

2. Self-educate.

We rarely have adequate information to know and execute every action step required to achieve our goals. The most important investment we can make in our lifetimes is in developing ourselves. Mastering the topic or area of interest that can guide us to our goal increases our ability to define and execute decisive action steps to maximize successful outcomes.

As you prepare to take on your goal, identify five or more resources that can provide an abundance of information to guide you from start to finish. Here are some ideas:

- Read topical references and how-to books.
- Watch informative videos.
- Consult with subject matter experts.
- Connect with a knowledgeable mentor.
- Attend classes or online courses.
- Invest into a MasterClass.
- View webinars.

Educate yourself by selecting quality and unbiased information from sources that align with your learning style. For some of us, online courses may provide information that we can digest. For others, we may read books, attend classes, and watch videos to help us define action steps to achieve the goal. Reach out to those who have been successful at what you would like to accomplish. Take the seeds of their wisdom and throw away the fruit. The fruit results from their success, but the seeds are for you to grow your knowledge and vision. If your goal is to make a documentary film, investing in a MasterClass instructed by an expert documentary filmmaker, such as Ken Burns, postures you to define action steps that can take you further than envisioned. Surround yourself with thinkers and believers with similar ambitions. If you surround yourself with doubters, then your doubt will grow. Be who you want to be by choice and not by the opinions or influences of others.

Analyze the information and dialogue that you allow to enter your inner body. Form your own opinions and invite others to question your beliefs. You will understand what you don't know but need to know. If you want greatness in all areas of your life, it starts with challenges and information. The more you know about your manifestation, goal, or desire, the less doubt will be present. Doubt creates limitations. The intention, without a doubt, drives success. Growth does not occur without knowing how to grow from experiences. Get the information you need to change your reality. Educate and develop yourself, and you'll stand tall like an oak tree. You may experience scrapes and scars, but even the most brutal winds will be no match for the depth of knowledge and confidence that provides you strength.

3. Develop an action plan with intention.
Just like setting goals with intention and purpose, intention and meaning should be at the root of your action-planning steps. Destiny begins with intentions, and it's the actions that take you there. Success comes from what we do intentionally and consistently. Without a plan of action that reflects your intentions, your goal and efforts will fall short of your expectations. When your beliefs are strong, your emotions will be strong, your actions will be decisive, and success will come to you! You are in complete control of how successful you are at anything.

Develop your manifested goals and desires by researching to understand what it takes for you to achieve success. Understand why you are seeking success. Visualize a successful outcome and consider the path it took to get there. Actions change the impossible to possible, but you have to be in a positive, productive state of mind that is clear and driven by knowing you are highly favored to succeed.

Begin the action-planning steps by listing all the action steps to achieve your goal. Some steps will be steps within steps, so write those down too. The order or timing of the action steps should not be a concern at this point. We want to avoid shortcuts and consider all the possible details to get us to where we want to be. The more complete the list, the more accurate the action plan will be when ordering and prioritizing the steps.

Organize the steps in an optimal order that prioritizes what needs to happen sooner before other efforts take place. Create the action plan with flexibility, solid milestones and realistic dates, that will guide you. Reflect on the plan as it comes together and ask yourself repeatedly, does this plan reflect my intentions? If not, think deeper and make changes. The plan itself is crucial, but what the plan means to you is more important. Create the plan based on your vision and creativity. Allow space for aligned opportunities to bring you even closer to the goal. When you give anything meaning, you feel differently and therefore move differently. Be aware and adaptable. Think of the action plan as a guiding tool to drive emotion and motivate as you engage each step toward progress and achievement. Success is in the journey. Commit to the journey, and intentional success can be yours.

4. Execute the action plan with self-discipline.

Self-discipline is the ability to stay on track toward a goal, no matter what may tempt us to go off track. It's at the foundation of anything worth having or achieving. Self-discipline is neutralizing near-term pleasures to align with or remain on the path of your desire.

Begin by removing things from your space that distract or disrupt, executing intentional actions toward your goal. Make choices ahead of time, leaving nothing up to chance. If your goal is to continue education and broaden your skills, taking on additional social responsibilities may not align with your intentions. Develop sustainable mini-habits that align with your goal. If you want to lose weight, eat at a healthy restaurant with healthy food choices you enjoy. You are the sole facilitator of change in your life, and change only occurs is if you are in control of yourself. Change is possible when we carry out our decisions through self-disciplined action.

5. Commit to your action plan.

An action plan with thoughtful steps drives deliberate and intentional action toward your goal. Commit to your action plan by removing and minimizing distractions or disruptions of progress. If you know you have a weakness of falling off task, consider stopgaps you can put in place that will help you refocus. A stopgap may be to review your vision board or watch an inspiring video about your goal. Create new daily habits centered on the pathway toward your goal, such as a dedicated time of day to work on your goal. The more authentically you connect with each step, the easier it becomes to be committed and execute the goal intended.

For many of us, commitment has a negative vibe or leads to feelings of FOMO (Fear Of Missing Out). Are you *really* missing out or just need perspective? Instead of thinking of commitment as negative or giving up something, think of commitment as freeing yourself from limiting behaviors and enabling yourself to create habits in alignment with happiness and success. Understand that success comes to those who position themselves for success. What are you doing to be successful? You have the power of choice and can choose to be successful. Take advantage of the greatness inside of you and execute only intentional actions that lead to success.

We can think, visualize, and talk about what we desire, but nothing worthy happens until intentional action occurs. We interact with 80,000 or more people in a lifetime, assuming an age of 78.5 years old.[12] Suppose 1,000 people died without putting their dreams into action, and each of their dreams would have positively

12 Irma Wallace, "Why We Live: Counting the People Your Life Impacts," Infographic Journal, May 3, 2013, https://infographicjournal.com/why-we-live-counting-the-people-your-life-impacts.

impacted 100,000 people. If we do the math, 100,000,000 people may have achieved tremendous success in their life if the original 1,000 people had realized their dreams. The value we contribute by achieving intentional success is greater than self.

Michael Jordan's dream was to win national championships. He aligned his passion for basketball with his actions to realize his dream and became one of the greatest players of all time. Without MJ realizing his dream, would LeBron James or the late Kobe Bryant be the accomplished players they came to be? Would MJ's teammates have played at the level demanded to win six championships without MJ's influence? How many people did MJ's teammates influence because of their respective national championship journeys?

Focus and success are contagious. The compounding effects of our actions ripple infinitely through society. Charles Barkley once said, "I'm not a role model. Just because I dunk a basketball doesn't mean I should raise your kids." Whether Barkley knew it or not, kids were paying attention, and his contributions through his successes were impacting millions and millions of lives. Barkley didn't make the varsity team during his junior year of high school. If he had given up his basketball aspirations, we would not know the NBA and Olympian superstar Charles Barkley. Many of us would not have been inspired by his "I can do anything" attitude. Intentional action delivers success for us and inspires thought and action for others.

We never know who's looking up to us as an idol or role model. We don't know how the simplest of our actions today will affect the complexity of outcomes tomorrow. Action is at the intersection of where we are and where we want to be. To progress toward where we want to be, we must cross the intersection with action.

There will be times when the action we take is not impactful or doesn't lead to the results we expect. Forced action led by ego can lead to negative results if the motivations and actions misalign with our intentions. Having the self-awareness to take actions that move us toward success takes practice and is mastered with time. Disappointments or missteps are feedback signals to affirm our beliefs and provide opportunities for redirection. Feedback teaches us lessons that success never will. Plan and execute actions with intention, and success shows up greater than your expectations.

TIME FOR REFLECTION

To help prepare me pursue my goal, I intend to:

I intend to prioritize the following responsibilities:

I intend to dedicate time toward achieving my goal by:

Five resources that align with how I learn and digest information are:

The necessary action steps to achieve my goal are:

To help me achieve self-discipline, I intend to:

CHAPTER SEVENTEEN

Spread Your Wings, Butterfly

"We delight in the beauty of the butterfly, but rarely admit the changes it has gone through to achieve that beauty."
—Maya Angelou

A 5K ROAD race is my favorite distance race when competing in run exhibitions. They are a tad more than three miles, short and sweet, depending on perspective and physical conditioning. As a 5K race competitor, I set measurable and quantifiable goals for race days, such as an average pace and a completion time. The 5K race is a mid-distance sprint. There isn't much time or distance between the start and finish lines to get back to the game plan if I'm not mentally and physically executing the race as intended.

My passion for 5K races connected me with a local fitness gym with a run club. You may recall, I joined the run club as a runner and became a run coach. Well, I led their Couch to 5K training program soon after. The program provided training and guidance to walkers and novice runners to achieve their 5K race goals. The following race season, I received an offer to coach a marathon (26.2 miles) training program. Since I had coached only 5K runners, completed one half-marathon (13.1 miles) road race, and never considered running a marathon, I was hesitant to accept the challenge. Compared to the preferred three-mile races, I had always thought twenty-six-mile races were for crazy people. (Note the limiting belief. After some soul-searching, I accepted the offer to lead the marathon training program.

To prepare for the program, I consulted with and received guidance from seasoned marathon race coaches. I read long-distance elite runners' memoirs, watched long-distance road races, met with nutritionists and injury prevention specialists, and ran with long-distance runners on their training runs. I even learned the origin and history of the word *marathon*, which made superb storytelling at cocktail parties. Marathon training and running had become my life. I became the running subject matter expert and authentically connected with the runners once the program began. To my amazement, my communication style and coaching ability inspired the runners to believe in their capabilities beyond their perceived limitations. The runners ran further on long-distance runs and faster during speed workouts than ever before. My confidence as a run coach grew as I witnessed runners developing their skills and overcoming limiting beliefs day by day.

The program concluded, and runners competed in the target race, exceeding their goals. As the marathon race season closed, I reflected on the experience and felt accomplished as a coach. I also felt accomplished as a runner. During the training program, I ran more miles than I ever thought possible, refined my diet with foods that support long-distance running, and practiced self-care like never before. Suddenly running a 26.2-mile road race no longer seemed like a crazy idea.

The following year, I trained for my first-ever marathon, the Richmond Marathon hosted in Richmond, Virginia. I relied heavily on the knowledge and techniques learned and applied during the training program to train for the race adequately. I had one goal: to cross the finish line.

Each week, I executed training sessions with specific training outcomes, such as distance, speed, and recovery. There was little to no energy or thought directed toward completing the marathon after setting the goal. I was confident that if I focused on and completed every training session as intended, I would finish the race. I developed as a stronger runner with each training session as I aligned my thoughts and actions with an elite marathon runner's mindset. Some weeks I ran fifty miles. Other weeks, I ran over seventy miles. Regardless of the distance, I practiced being mindfully present during each mile and monitoring my thoughts and body with every step. I didn't worried about the last mile, the mile ahead, or how far I had left to go. Training for a 26.2-mile race differs from training for a three-mile race, but the mindset is the same—be present and execute as planned.

On race day, after completing my pre-race routine, I focused on being one with the race atmosphere. I visualized an exciting race, waved to spectators, and sang the National Anthem as I claimed a spot behind the start line among the thousands of eager runners. All the hard work and training were complete. The Richmond Marathon was the first time I had lined up behind a starting line without a completion time in mind. I was living in the moment, not the outcome. My mind was calm, body relaxed. Why worry about the outcome? As we know, manifestations work when we let go of the desired result. It was time to execute every mile to the best of my ability. I was ready to give it my all and had no concern about anything else.

The start gun blasted, and the race started without a hitch. Some runners quickly skipped out ahead of the crowd, while other runners let the race come to them. As I settled into a comfortable pace and navigated around slower runners, I joined a runner pack running a similar speed. When we pace with other runners, we avoid running too fast, too early in the race. We were like a pack of wolves migrating through a paved forest of people as a cohesive unit for miles one through eight. The novice to intermediate runners fell to the middle and rear ranks as the seasoned runners led the charge. As we made our way through miles nine and ten, I separated from the pack by ever so slightly increasing my speed. I felt strong and better than I could ever imagine at this point in the race. My race plan was working, and it was time to spread my wings.

I ran the remaining miles mindfully, fully engaged with each mile one by one. If there was a hill, I maintained effort. If there was a water stop, I strategically found a path to access the water without slowing down. My trust in my abilities to push harder grew as I surpassed mile after mile. By mile twenty-one, I passed runners who scooted by me during the first few miles. With over five miles left to run and fatigue setting like the weight of a ship's anchor. I asked myself, *How badly do you want it, Coombs?* For some reason, my inner voice has always been that of a military drill sergeant. Go figure. I may need to unpack that. I refocused on the mile at hand and pushed the pace faster, passing more runners.

I released any thoughts of failure and focused on breathing. *Breathe, Coombs. Breathe.* We talk a lot to ourselves during a 26.2-mile race. Maybe we marathoners are crazy after all. The mind cleared, running form improved. The redirecting of thought confirmed that the mind controls the physical body and not the other way around. As I approached the last mile and a half stretch of asphalt, entering a corridor of thunderous spectating cheers, I felt the urge to dig deeper and run faster. I passed three more runners. *You got this, Coombs.* I mentally thrust myself into 5K race mode to sprint through to the finish. I'm not sure if I physically ran any faster, but mentally it felt as if I were on wheels. As I made my way closer toward the finish line, my legs wobbled, and my feet screamed for mercy. It didn't matter. Nothing was going to stop me now.

I unleashed the inner beast with everything I had and toe-tapped across the finish line of my first-ever marathon. With uncontrollable rolling tears filled with emotions, I received a marathon finisher medal. I finished the race in three hours, three minutes, and within the top 3 percent of total race finishers. Spectating runners and traveling run club members congratulated me on qualifying for the Boston Marathon, the unicorn of marathons, as I exited the finish line chute.

Wait, what? What does the Boston Marathon have to do with the Richmond Marathon? I did not know the Richmond Marathon was a Boston Marathon–qualifying race or marathon runners had to qualify to enter the Boston Marathon. Who knew? Not this guy. Two years later, I trained for and completed the Boston Marathon on Patriots Day.

The story above is an example of how we can overcoming limiting beliefs can lead to a favorable outcome beyond the imagination. It's also a story that shows how we can invite abundance when we intentionally deliver our highest value. If we don't open our minds beyond our limiting beliefs and perceptions, we cannot unleash intentional success. Let me explain.

As a 5K runner, I was content with running a race that I knew well and finishing among the top runners in my age group. Running 3.1 miles is incomparable, mentally and physically, to running 26.2 miles—a mental block. I had a subconscious limiting belief that marathon runners were far more talented and mentally stronger runners than I was, so I referred to them as crazy. That's ego, the judge. Are you judging others based on your limitations? I was comfortable in the 5K race lane, which limited my potential as a runner and in life. Coaching the marathon training program and training for a marathon launched a growth journey released me from limiting beliefs. Accepting a challenge, opening my mind, doing the work, and detaching from perceived limitations has increased my life's success.

Are there things that you tell yourself to make yourself comfortable with where you are? Are you waiting for everything to be in place before pursuing a goal or advancing to the next step? To achieve our goals, we must choose progress over procrastination and perfection. I accepted the challenge of coaching something I knew little about instead of waiting on perfect timing or until I had enough expertise to feel confident for such an undertaking. If you want something, you will discover ways to succeed with a success mindset followed by intentional actions. Accepting challenges make us uncomfortable but can inspire exponential growth. Growth begins when you let go of limiting beliefs and open your mind to new opportunities and limitless possibilities.

When we are mindfully aware, we understand that success may come in forms that we may not recognize. Where would I be today if I had not accepted the coaching opportunity? Would my decisions, ego, and mindset be able to push beyond other perceived limitations without the coaching and marathon experiences? The tears that fell at the finish of the Richmond Marathon were not tears of pain or even joy. The tears were an emotional release of acceptance that my life will never be the same again. I didn't give up or let the physical and mental stress of running a marathon beat me down as each mile became excruciating to endure.

Success was not at the finish line. The victory was in the planning, training, and execution leading up to the enlightening moment of crossing the finishing line.

With each step and thought during training and the race, I progressed forward toward my goal. The successful outcome is not that I completed the race. The successful result is that I ran each of the 26.2 miles to the best of my ability—the only part of the race I could control.

My longest training run was eighteen miles, occurring only once, and 8.2 miles shy of a marathon's length. Running is 90 percent mindset. I could have run slower, stopped along the course, injured myself, or even quit. Instead, I found the courage to keep going. Do you have the courage to keep going? Or do you give up when challenges seem too significant? I left a shell of myself on the racecourse that day by replacing layers of limiting beliefs and challenging myself to push beyond the borders of my imagination. I left Richmond grateful and confident that nothing can cap success once I have set a goal, planned aligned actions, and execute actions intentionally. There are far greater things in store for us than we can perceive. We have to believe with every ounce of our beings that we can receive everything we deserve. Are you aware of doorways and opportunities of abundance as they appear? Do you have the mindfulness to notice when your gateway for growth has arrived?

We make thousands of decisions based on subconsciously downloaded information that feeds our thoughts and beliefs. The information we process either elevates or limits our decisions and actions depending on the quality and nature of the information received. Our innate negative bias can negatively feed the ego, triggering self-doubt. We must practice vulnerability and self-awareness to empower ourselves to know where we are emotionally and mentally as we go through life. If we master our emotions, thoughts, and actions, we will experience our most abundant lives. Every emotion drives thought. Every thought has a vibrational frequency that can positively or negatively drive our efforts and actions.

Once we understand where we are within, we can make prosperous decisions with trust and confidence in our abilities to plan with intention and execute purposeful actions. Neutralizing ego and responding with clarity to a marathon coaching opportunity led to two marathon races and changed the trajectory of happiness and success in my life. Who saw that coming? To see the offer as a passage for immense growth, I had to detach myself from limiting influences, observations, and experiences that fueled negative energy and framed my my thoughts about marathons. I had to release jealously, resentment, and judgment against marathon runners and empty my container for abundance. It was not until I had let go of my inhibitions I could see myself coaching marathon runners.

Do you only engage in activities that make you feel comfortable? Are your thoughts and actions reflective of your values? We expand success in our lives when we create boundaries based on our values and let go of constraints on our ideas, thoughts, and actions. To be successful in any life area, we have to understand and validate the origins of our thoughts and actions. Are limiting beliefs and thoughts driving your decisions and actions? Have limiting beliefs become your reality? You are capable of intentionally unleashing yourself for better outcomes.

UNLEASH INTENTIONAL SUCCESS

Our wellness expands our level of happiness and success. Being mentally, emotionally, and physically healthy prepares and supports our growth by providing a good foundation for higher vibrational energy, positive thought, and elevated productivity. We invite more favorable outcomes into our lives without wellness walls or blocks. Unhealthy states of mind such as anger, stress, resentment, or partaking in alcohol and substance abuse deter abundance and bottleneck happiness and success. You can position yourself to unleash intentional success with a few simple steps.

1. Develop emotional vulnerability and practice self-awareness.

Few of us are both emotionally vulnerable and self-aware. To improve either, we have to work on both intentionally. Emotional vulnerability is the willingness to show up as you are and recognize your emotions, thoughts, and weaknesses instead of shunning or suppressing. Some of us disguise our fears as blame, judgment, resentment, or anger to protect ourselves from appearing weak or avoid taking full responsibility for our experiences. Having emotional vulnerability allows us to overcome blocks that limit how we understand ourselves, connect with others, and expand our imagination. Transformation or change can only begin once we know where we are and where we want to be.

Do you have a temper? Why? Are you aware that you have fears that drive your actions and reactions? What are you protecting? Until you become emotionally vulnerable and let go of your worries, you are a frigid shadow of yourself. Brené Brown, an American professor, said, "Vulnerability is not winning or losing; it's having the courage to show up and be seen when we have no control over the outcome." The less we are authentic, the less we can be our happiest, and the less we experience maximized successful outcomes.

When we lack self-awareness, we react to situations and scenarios in ways that do not align with our values or in a manner that does not match the situation or scenario. Emotional vulnerability helps us understand our challenges, feelings, and motivations and unveils our inner selves. Self-awareness is about managing how we feel and aligning our thoughts and actions with our values. Being both emotionally vulnerable and self-aware enables us to be unbiased assessors of ourselves and minimize self-sabotaging behavior.

2. Let it go, mindfully.

Abundance begins within. Many of us cling to beliefs, people, agendas, and experiences that temporarily give us the feeling of happiness but ultimately hold us back. Why? What are you afraid of losing or missing? "If I get the next promotion, my life will be complete. If I get a new car, I will be happy. If I travel, I will be free." Getting a promotion, buying a new car, and traveling are great goals, but they should not define you or carry the responsibility of making you happy or fulfilled. Exist in a space where what you want happens as it should instead of forcing outcomes based on your timeline for happiness and success.

Time and time again, we learn that externally seeking happiness and fulfillment leaves insatiable voids. What happens when we have everything we desire but feel unfulfilled? Lasting satisfaction occurs when our source of joy comes from within, and we let go of what no longer adds value. Reaching for happiness leads to disappointment or temporary gratification. If we consider holding onto something in the physical sense, our grasp restricts us from moving forward. The same occurs when holding on to anything emotionally; we cannot progress forward. Letting go mindfully releases you from internal limitations or unnecessary worry in a balanced and accepting manner. Since human beings have existed, nothing has ever changed for the better with worry, yet we worry. What would happen if you let go? What would happen if you didn't let go?

Letting go provides emotional and mental freedom to perceive more remarkable outcomes. Suppressed negative feelings and thoughts encourage self-sabotaging behavior. If we live mindfully, our focus is on the present, free from the past's remorse or fear of the future—we attain a sense of liberation from mental burdens and gain peace in being. We see everything as it is, peacefully achieving clarity, focus, and abundance. A peaceful mind is a fertile mind for unlimited possibilities.

3. Consider and fully explore short, intermediate, and long-term purposeful goals.

When we establish goals, we should be mindful of why the goal matters to us. Is the goal based on your desires? Does the goal genuinely align with your values? How will the goal add value to your life or others' lives? Goal-setting without meaning or intention lacks the emotional connection necessary to drive thoughts and actions toward the goal. Setting intentional goals increases the will and motivation to commit to sustainable personal habits and tactics that can unearth aligned steps and shed light on opportunities to achieve the goal. It also means having fewer goals grants increased focus on each goal.

If you find difficulty relating to or seeing yourself achieving goals, a more in-depth evaluation of the goal's purpose may be necessary. Understanding why we want what we want and being specific on what we want redirects our thoughts and actions toward progress instead of being stuck in neutral.

4. Evolve your actions to reflect intentionally focused thought. Many of us set goals, but our efforts detract, stall, or marginalize our dreams' outcomes. It takes intention, self-discipline, and confidence to transition from being a dreamer to an achiever. We should plan and execute our actions with a crystal-clear motive for the expected accomplishment. Why does the action step make sense? How does the action step align with your values and goals? Is there something you could do today to maximize the results of your actions? The more you practice being deliberate with all your efforts, the more contributive and intuitive your actions become.

As you consider the next action step, stay in the present and examine the highest value activity you could do to place yourself a step closer to your goal. Success arrives with mindful execution of the highest valued actions. Value occurs when our efforts align with our core principles and deliver our best for ourselves and others. We want to avoid overthinking or creating anxiety about the outcome of our actions by mindfully framing our thoughts and minimizing distractions that can dilute the focus. Perfection and procrastination lead to idleness. Idleness costs us time! Choose progress by fulfilling a simple task in line with your goal. You may find yourself rejuvenated to complete additional tasks or inspired to ride the momentum wave to perform more impactful action steps. Revisit your plan and refine your goals as your conscious awareness and trust in the process increase. Uncertainty is okay, and challenges will remain, but stay vigilant with your desires and consistent with aligning your emotions, mindset, and actions with your goals.

Many of us believe that permanent change is impossible, which is true if our flawed perceptions of reality stay the same. Change is temporary unless the underlying beliefs that lead to self-sabotaging behavior transform. You have to want to change and be willing to do the work from the inside out. If you are successful in transforming your mindset, the freedom to dream, feel, believe, and act beyond all foreseen possibilities awaits you on the other side.

When Mom and Dad told me at age four that I could be whoever I wanted to be, I should have looked within! I spent years searching and attaching myself to the likeness of others when who I wanted to be was the authentic person that lives within.

Answer the call for growth and overcome your limitations. Give yourself grace and let go of anything that does not align with your peace, joy, and happiness. Visualize your growth evolution as if it's happening. See yourself as whole and becoming successful in all areas of your life. What does that look like for you? Enjoy the process, live in the moment, and detach from the outcome. The more pleasure you find in doing an activity, the more likely you are to repeat the activity, embrace its benefits, and achieve consistency.

Unleashing intentional success, whether it's wellness, career, or financial, requires intentional growth and actions. Any successful transformation requires the reprogramming of the subconscious mind. This concept is foundational for intentional success. When we learn something new, we have to live it, see it, and believe it for our learnings to become our reality. Whether your goal is to master the art of poetry, leadership, or just be the very best version of you at all times, you have everything you need and want within you to unleash the success you desire. Don't go to the grave with your dreams, ambitions, and goals unrealized. Contribute value and inspire others to be excellent in their lives. Don't live a life of continual judgment, misplaced blame, and flawed beliefs. Make peace with the old you by letting go of the past and leaving all baggage at the door.

Do you struggle with achieving success? Are you struggling with discovering the steps required for a successful outcome? Do you procrastinate or stall progress from time to time? If the answer is yes to any or all of these questions, a support system can help. Establishing a high-quality support system is essential to managing progress and accountability toward our goals. A support system built on trust and mutual respect is necessary to promote self-discipline and challenge us to follow through with our objectives. My run coach and marathon journey would not have been possible without a support system aligned with my values and goals. As adults, it takes a village to help us achieve all we desire and maximize our potential. When we falter or self-sabotage, we can attribute our missteps to the ego, living in our heads, limiting beliefs, or a flawed sense of reality. Establish a support system that keeps you honest with yourself and influences limitless beliefs.

Professional coaching is a solutions-focused practice that encourages higher levels of awareness and growth. I've had a professional coach in my support system for a few years. The growth achieved in a single year would have taken me five or more years to accomplish, even with a perfectly executed plan. If we are unaware of our limiting beliefs, we cannot know how far we can go. A professional coach can be an integral part of your support system to evoke awareness to help you discover optimal solutions, overcome limiting beliefs, and achieve personal growth in specific areas of your life.

As a success coach, I help clients set goals, discover the optimal paths, and develop habits and tactics to achieve successful outcomes. There is an African proverb that says, "If you want to go quickly, go alone. If you want to go far, go together." Marathoners pace with other runners until the opportune time to take the lead.

How has going quickly and alone worked out for you? Are you where you should be, or have you limited yourself? Coaching sessions position and empower you to feel and see beyond the perceived mental peripheries that prevent or delay success and fulfillment. If we operate at our highest value and trust the process, we will be happy and successful in everything we do.

What does performing at your highest value look like?

Are you living your life based on your expectations?

From meditation to journaling, to visualization to action planning and execution, we have learned many practices within this book that can become habits and deliver us to intentional success pathways. Alfred Mercier, a French poet, once said, "What we learn with pleasure we never forget." Implement practices you enjoy, and they will become habits as you adapt to your new normal. If you don't want to journal before bed, don't force it. Find an enjoyable time for journaling that fits your lifestyle and schedule. When meditation feels like a chore, try coloring in a coloring book or engage in an activity with similar mindful benefits.

Did you pick this book to read, or did this book pick you? The butterfly cover design of this book is a visual representation of happiness, energy, and freedom. The butterfly sets the tone for your self-discovery and growth journey before you turn the first page. Butterflies signify new life, rebirth, and transformation. Consider the butterfly on the cover and words on the pages as your guide to unleashing success in your life. Accept the challenge and follow the monarch butterfly. Butterflies do not fly in straight lines. Uncertainty, distractions, and disruptions may lead to feedback and redirection. That's okay. Remain intentional with your beliefs, thoughts, and actions to be positioned to continue on the path toward success. You defined this moment. Embrace it. It is your time to be the person you would like to meet.

You have read another self-help book! What now? It's time for some action!

1. Review the Time For Reflection pages at the end of every chapter.
2. Select a chapter that guides you on a topic in your life today.
3. Go to namainecoombs.com and sign up to receive bonus materials to help you get started.

Trees flourish from their roots, and so do we. If our values are bendable or our beliefs are invalid, growth and successful outcomes are limited. Rediscover yourself, set intentions, and gain focus by developing an awareness of who you are and what you want. Believe it, see it, and act on it, and the success you seek is already yours. Develop positive daily habits and lean on a sustainable support system. Project out into the world what you would like to receive. The positive contributions to yourself and others compound when you feel, believe and act in alignment with your values and goals. Create boundaries and live with a success mindset and you will unleash intentional success!

Acknowledgments

WRITING THIS BOOK was cognitively therapeutic and a telling of a hero's journey. Without the guidance, support, and encouragement of personal messengers, mentors, and champions, none of this would have been possible. Thank you to Dad and Mom, also known as Courtney and Joan Coombs, who raised and gave their children the best of their ability. This book and my life are full of fruitful experiences because of them. Dad guided me to be a gentleman, do my best always, take responsibility for the outcomes in my life, wholeheartedly pay attention, and not sacrifice today for tomorrow's hopes. Mom showed me how to be nonjudgmental and connected, love abundantly, and only take actions that provide peace. For my procreators, I am eternally grateful!

Thank you to my younger siblings, Kareem and Andrew, for inspiring me to lead by example, have patience, forgive purely, and, most importantly, that sharing is caring. Each one of us is different, but somehow, we are the same.

I am grateful to my grandparents, Solomon and Cynthia Werdenie, for teaching me to assume people are doing the best they can and to help others when in need. Grandma Pearl, for showing me God and why we should commit to our values and create boundaries.

Special thanks go to Uncle Morris, who questions everything and believes limitlessly, and the late Uncle Chubby, who practiced patience and optimism over everything.

We try to learn and be more for ourselves and others. Without understanding who we are, we are not able to see who we can be. Thank you to my former wife and dear friend, Melonie Coombs, for her persistent nudge to address my internal struggles with a therapist's help and her unwavering support throughout this journey. She is the definition of unconditional love.

Thank you to the Jamaican neighbors, Mercan, Joyce, Hopi, and Radcliff, who shared their gratitude and joy for the simplest things in life.

Shoutout to the original Dream Team: Gregory Brown, Chris Howard, Ta'Wayne Davis, and Carl Weston. We raised and inspired each other to become the great men we are today! We make our dreams come true. A special shoutout goes to GB for riding with me and providing perspective when I needed it the most.

Great friends like Odell McPherson, Waddell Sheppard, Ron G., Stefan Collado, and Kenny Goodwin are challenging to find. Each of them is a student of life, and I am grateful for our many conversations and moments of reflection.

Thank you to Minal Patel, Carlos Stennis, and Hazlitt Gill for faithfully being there and supporting me through the most significant inflection point of my life.

So grateful for my good friend and accountability partner, Melody Gross. She has been a fantastic accountability partner by holding me accountable for the actions that enabled my writing, speaking, and coaching dreams to become realities.

We can intentionally invite people into our lives without realizing how impactful they will be to us. Therapist Tammy Broadaway uncovered the roots of my limiting beliefs and self-sabotaging behavior. Former run club coaches James Fisher and Lewis Messina introduced me to run coaching and marathon running—experiences that forever changed my life. Thank you all.

To my mentor, Ty Smith, who challenged me to evaluate and broaden my perceived reality to experience exceptional outcomes. I am grateful for you.

To the founding board of directors at UpROAR Leadership Academy, Genesia Newsome, Wes Farnam, Benjy Stephens, Tim Stroman, Scott Graykowski, Brooke Adamson, and LaToya Purvis: I am so thankful for the trust placed in my ability to lead an organization from the idea phase to producing thriving cadet-scholars.

Finally, I am grateful for you and all those who have been instrumental in getting here: Leon Stepherson, Coach Cayme, Michelle Samuel-Foo, and Nora McCormack. We are better together, and it has genuinely taken a village.

About the Author

Namaine Coombs is a certified professional life coach and an established financial professional. As a military brat, he was raised in West Point, New York, and Columbia, South Carolina, by his lovely Jamaican parents. He holds a BS in business administration, an MBA in finance, and a Chartered Financial Analyst (CFA) designation. He is also a member of the International Coaching Federation (ICF), the National Alliance of Mental Illness (NAMI), and an advocate for mental health. He gets excited over German cars, keeps his body healthy by running, and travels to warm destinations as often as possible. Namaine lives in Charlotte, North Carolina, where he visualizes being taller on a daily basis. He is the author of *Unleash Intentional Success.*

Connect with the Author

namainecoombs.com
instagram.com/namainecoombs
twitter.com/namainecoombs
info@namainecoombs.com

Leave a Review

If you enjoyed reading *Unleash Intentional Success*, will you consider writing a review on your platform of choice? Reviews help indie authors find more readers like you.

www.ingramcontent.com/pod-product-compliance
Lightning Source LLC
Chambersburg PA
CBHW030822090426
42737CB00009B/837
* 9 7 8 1 7 3 4 6 8 8 9 1 7 *